I0477603

The Small Business Guide to: Market Planning

How to Create Winning Strategies to Conquer Your Market

Nicholas L. Peoples

The Small Business Guide to: Market Planning
Self-Published 2018
First Edition

Library of Congress Cataloging in Publication Data
ISBN 978-1-64153-206-8
Peoples, Nicholas L.
The Small Business Guide to: Market Planning

PRINTED IN THE UNITED STATES OF AMERICA

TO MY CHILDREN, Nick Jr., Julian, and Arielle who give me a reason to be great. To my family who kept believing in me through it all. I love you.

CONTENTS

Introduction...xi

Section One: Back to Basics.............................1

Chapter 1: What is Market Planning? 3

Path to Profitability 3

What is a Marketing Plan? 5

Marketing Wars..5

Market Planning for Small Business 6

Objectives and Goals...7

Chapter 2: Marketing 101 9

Marketing Basics..9

Marketing Management Philosophies...................10

The Marketing Mix 11

Marketing Mix Strategies 12

Segment the Market...13

Find Your Target 18

Positioned for Success 20

Consumer vs. Business-to-Business Marketing ...22

Marketing Goods vs. Marketing Services 24

Chapter 3: The Do-it-Yourself Marketing Plan.........29

What Your Marketing Consultant Doesn't Want You to Know
....29

Collecting the Right Information...........................30

Turning Data into Knowledge...............................32

Organize Your Findings 33

Strategic Management..34

Use Your Imagination 37

Section Two: Creating your Marketing Plan 39

Overview: 40

Chapter 4: Marketing Plan Part One *Company Description* 41

History 41

How You Got Started 42

Corporate Values 42

The Purpose You Serve...43

Previous Marketing Strategies 43

Other Historical Facts 43

The Organization Today 44

How Your Company Has Changed............................44

Company Types...44

Company Image...45

Business Model...46

Business Mission 46

The Product You Offer 47

The Problem You Solve/Need you Fulfill 47

Your System of Operation......................................48

Differentiation 49

Projected Future 49

Market Positioning 52

Revenues...53

Profits..56

Product Mix 57

Market Share 58

Chapter 5: Marketing Plan Part Two *Market Analysis* 61

Situational Analysis...62

Finding Your Competitive Advantage 66

Cost...67

Product/Service Differentiation 67

Niche Strategy 68

Sustainable Competitive Advantages 68

Market Research..69

Market Status..70

Market Size 70

Market Value..71

Your Share of the Market..72

Trends..73

Product Life-Cycle..74

Competition..75

Market Testing 76

Market Tests 77

Consumer Tests..78

Company Capabilities Test 79

Analyzing Market Information 80

Chapter 6: Marketing Plan Part Three *Marketing Mix*..............85

Product Strategy 86

Product Development 86

Product Mix 87

Packaging 88

Branding..90

Quality Assurances 91

Positioning 91

Place (Distribution) Strategy 92

Service Area 93

Supply Chain Management..94

Logistics 96

Price Strategy 97

Costs..97

Market Value..102

Competitive Pricing 104

Other Factors 105

Chapter 7: Marketing Plan Part Four: *Define Target Market* ..107

  Divide up the Market 108

    Choose Segmentation Bases 109

    Segmentation in Action 111

  Select Your Target 112

  Profile Your Target 113

    Describe Them 114

    Rank Them 115

  Best Communication Methods 116

Chapter 8: Marketing Plan Part Five: *Communication Plan* ...118

  Designing Campaigns 119

    Themes 119

    Communication Objectives 120

    Message Clarity 121

    Supporting the Theme 122

  Using the AIDA Model 123

    Attention 124

    Interest 124

    Desire 125

    Action 125

    Applying AIDA 126

  Promotion Mix 126

    Public Relations 127

    Advertising 132

    Sales Promotion 136

  Integrating Promotional Elements 138

  Other Promotional Mix Considerations 139

    Overall Cost 139

    Cost Per Contact 140

    Reach 141

    Frequency 141

    Audience Selectivity 142

Communication Strategy.......................................143

Writing the Communication Plan..........................144

Chapter 9: Marketing Plan Part Six *Competition* 146

Who are Your Competitors? 146

Location 147

Key Players...147

Philosophy/Vision..148

Additional Info. 148

Research Their Operation...................................148

Finding Competitive Intelligence 148

Analyze the Competitors' Product.........................150

Size Them Up 151

How They Sell Their Offerings 153

Evaluate Their Operation 154

Competitive Strategy.......................................156

Product Differentiation 156

Stealing Away Market Share..............................157

Handling Threats...158

Exploiting Weaknesses....................................159

Chapter 10: Marketing Plan Part Seven *Sales Plan* 161

Selling Methods 162

Procedure 163

Generating Leads 164

Pre-Sale Techniques 165

Sales Pitch 167

Sale Closing Strategies....................................168

Post-Sale Techniques......................................169

Sales Team..170

Your Sales Goals 172

Chapter 11 Marketing Plan Part Eight: *Cash Flow Statements and Budgets*...175

Cash Flow Basics 176

    More Than Just Paper 176

    How does Cash Flow Work?....................................176

    Positive and Negative 177

They Work Together 178

Net-Positive Cash Flow..178

Cash Flow Statements...180

Budgeting..182

Staying on Budget...187

Introduction

Starting a small business is not easy. There is usually a large amount of hard work, many early mornings, and countless late nights. There are more ups downs than a nauseating amusement park ride. You must invest time, money, blood, sweat, and tears to even have a chance at success, yet you still want to be "your own boss." Understandably so, because the potential payoffs can exceed your wildest dreams!

For small business owners, business success leads directly to personal success. Not only do you get the satisfaction of knowing that you have built a thriving enterprise, but you also get the money! Being the owner of a profitable and prosperous business can bring you what you elude so many of us; financial freedom! True financial freedom means no more living paycheck-to-paycheck. When you no longer have to worry about how you will pay the bills and can spend what you want when you want, you have become financially free! Achieving financial freedom is the whole point of becoming a small business owner. It is the reward for all of the risks you are taking.

Since your personal wealth is so closely tied to your business, you want to do whatever it takes to succeed. By purchasing this manual, you have taken a step in the right direction. Market planning is the catalyst between where your business is and where you need it to be.

Located within these pages is everything you need to know about market planning. You will learn how to analyze your market, recognize the trends, and build strategies to capitalize. Using an easy-to-understand style, this manual will guide you through the fundamentals of marketing and show you how to apply them to your planning efforts.

The **Small Business Guide to: Market Planning** is based upon extensive research and expert knowledge. Thousands of pages of marketing information have been condensed into this single volume. It is designed to be easily read and cater specifically to the needs of the small business owner. After reading this manual, you will be confident in your market planning abilities and ready to take your business to the next level.

This manual isn't about gimmicks and empty promises of prosperity overnight. These are sound processes and procedures that will bring you long-term success. If you are willing to sacrifice the time and effort to do things right, the **Small Business Guide to: Market Planning** will show you how to turn your business into a profit-generating machine.

Section One:
Back to Basics

Chapter 1:
What is Market Planning?

S tarting a business without a plan is like driving a car at night without headlights...You can't see where you are going. You may generally be headed in the right direction, but you can't see the obstacles right in front of you. If you are lucky enough to survive without crashing, you may find that in the darkness you have veered off your path and lost your way.

In this chapter, we shine a light on the path to profitability, find out exactly what a marketing plan is, explore the importance of market planning to small business, and accurately define objectives and goals. Upon completion of this chapter, you should have an excellent understanding of the market planning aspect of business management.

Path to Profitability

Why do we go into business? Is it to create jobs for others? Maybe it's the chance to do what we love every day. Could it be we desire to share our vision with the world? All of these are feasible--even noble--secondary reasons to be in business, but the primary reason we are all in business is to make profits. That is objective number one!

Most business owners measure success by the amount of profit that they made over a period. The further you get beyond the break-even-point, the better you have done in that period. Profits are what allow you the ability to either fatten your bank account or reinvest in your company. You need to make money to stay in business. You need to make money to grow your business.

So, where do profits come from? Well, we know they don't just fall out of the sky, and since the mythical profit tree continues to elude discovery, we must look elsewhere. Profits are born out of revenues, also known as positive cash flow. Before you can make profits, cash flows must exist. Cash flow is the movement of cash into and out of a business. Of course, more money coming in than going out constitutes a positive cash flow.

You can create continuous and consistent positive cash flow on your own. What this means is you can affect your company's cash flows directly. You don't have to be lucky (although it helps) because positive cash flow is ultimately created through marketing. Effective marketing can transform a stagnating small business into a revenue-generating giant. Effective marketing can transform a struggling adolescent company into a stable, mature enterprise. Marketing is your most powerful tool for creating positive cash flow.

Planning enhances the effectiveness of your marketing efforts. The more carefully you plan your marketing activities, the better chance they will prove fruitful. With proper planning, you will gain a vast amount of insight into your market. With this insight, you will be able to deeply penetrate the market and command an outstanding share of it. Therefore, market planning is the key to profitability.

Now, let's retrace our steps and reveal the path to profitability. Profits are derived from positive cash flows. To create positive cash flow, you need effective marketing. Marketing is most effective when it is carefully thought out and planned. Therefore, market planning is our first, and most important, step in the path to profitability.

What is a Marketing Plan?

Every organization has objectives for each component of their business. Meeting these objectives takes some planning. You must plan in anticipation for future events; you must plan to determine strategies. Market planning involves designing the activities related to the marketing objectives of your organization. You use a written document called a marketing plan to organize your market planning efforts. The marketing plan funnels all the information, insight, ideas, and knowledge that you have collected into a highly concentrated strategic weapon.

Every marketing plan is unique. There is no single formula for creating one. There are some common elements among all marketing plans though. Every marketing plan should contain a business mission, company objectives, a market analysis, establishment of the marketing mix components, and a definition of your target market. You can enhance your plan with a myriad of other elements such as budgets, evaluation measures, or timelines for implementation.

It is important to note that the marketing plan is not just a consecutive series of planning steps. Each element stands alone, but they must work in conjunction to meet your organizational marketing objectives. When making decisions about one component, you must consider all the other parts as well. A marketing plan that is cohesive and uniform ensures you get the best results

Marketing Wars

Picture for a moment your company as an army in a marketing war. Your competitors are, well...Your competitors. They want to win just as bad as you; they have just as much at stake as you. Let's face it; your livelihood is on the line here. This is how you eat. You can't afford to lose!

The market is your battleground, and you must fight hard to

maintain control of your share. To gain a more significant share, you must fight even harder and smarter. That larger share you seek will usually belong to someone else, and the owners are going to defend it fiercely. To conquer and control your desired percentage of the market, you must have a bigger army with more ammunition (resources) or develop a superior strategy by carefully planning your attacks.

Since you probably don't have the luxury of seemingly limitless resources like some of your larger competitors, you must focus your efforts on strategy if you want to win. That's where the marketing plan comes into play; it's your secret weapon. Advance knowledge of the battlefield (the market) gives you the ability to outmaneuver your opponent and gain an advantage. Your marketing plan provides you with a map of the market and serves as the guidebook that lays out the marketing activities your organization will engage in. Base your strategy on a solid marketing plan, and you'll come out on top when the smoke clears.

Market Planning for Small Business

Most small business owners can't afford to waste a dime on marketing activities that are ineffective. Your marketing budget is usually much smaller than the big players in the field which means that your margin of error is much lower as well. You must be more careful, concise, and calculating with each marketing dollar you spend. Writing a marketing plan will help you to Maximize your marketing budget by keeping all activities on track and in line with your company's predetermined objectives.

Market planning can level the playing field for your small business. Your larger counterparts may have an entire marketing department whose sole job is to analyze consumer behavior with complex formulas, or evaluate market trends using complicated computer algorithms, but they usually lack the intimate knowledge of the market that you have. You are on the ground level of the market dealing with your customers every day. Your unique, more personal understanding of the market can be very valuable. Focus it with effective market planning, and you may find a sustainable competitive advantage.

For those who are still trying to bring their business ideas to life, market planning can offer you a running start. The marketing plan is the most critical part of your business planning. Before entering a market, you want to be well-informed and ready. A business plan that includes a complete marketing plan gives your business the best chance to succeed.

Also, as a new business, you may need to acquire some start-up capital to get your business off the ground. You should know that investors don't care about your dream, they want to how you will make them money! Lenders aren't concerned with your contribution to society; they want to know how you will pay them back. When you present potential investors or lenders with a thorough marketing plan attached to your business plan, it shows them that you are well prepared and worthy of their funding.

Your marketing plan doesn't have to be a 100-page behemoth. It can be as simple as you want it to be as long as its complete. Your objectives should be well-defined, your information should be accurate, and your marketing activities should be clearly stated. Remember, you must devise your strategy based on this plan, so it needs to be as detailed as possible.

Objectives and Goals

The most important part of your market planning is determining what your objectives and goals are. These are vital decisions because they give direction to your marketing plan. You cannot develop the details of your plan until you know your marketing objectives. Base your marketing objectives on your company's overall business mission.

Marketing objectives are best defined as "The achievement

benchmarks upon which success of marketing activities can be measured." In other words, what exactly are you trying to achieve? You want to choose objectives that are realistic, measurable, and time specific. To say that you want to be the world market leader in beverage manufacturing is too vague, probably unrealistic for a small business, and has no time attachment. A more appropriate objective would be "To become the leader in local market share within 18 months"; or more specifically; "To increase market share by 25% in the local market in 12 months".

After determining your organization's marketing objectives, you can begin setting goals. Goals are the individual tasks that you must complete to accomplish your objectives. Your goals should be more specific than your objectives. Make your goals easily reachable and modest so that you can show yourself some progress. You will find that reaching goal after goal will give you great motivation. Before you know it, your business will be booming.

Marketing objectives and their corresponding goals are integral to your marketing plan. You will use the objectives as standards to measure your progress and keep you on track. Whenever you are wondering if you are headed in the right direction, ask yourself, "are we meeting our objectives?" and you'll know.

∞

We have discovered what a marketing plan is and why it is vital to the success of your small business. Our next step is formulating a plan. Before you begin writing though, let's give you a quick crash course in marketing. You'll find it helpful later.

Chapter 2:
Marketing 101

P ut that marketing textbook away! You don't need to be a marketing major to run a successful business. All you need to know is included right here in this chapter.

We will cover the fundamental aspects of marketing as it relates to your business. With a deeper understanding of these important marketing concepts, you will be able to develop an effective marketing plan our own.

<u>Marketing Basics</u>

We hear the term all the time, but what is marketing exactly? It is that commercial you hate so much but can't get out of your mind? Does it have anything to do with how products and services are made available to the consumer? Could it be the sales promotions, displays, and packaging that catch our attention persuading us to buy? Yes, marketing is a combination of all these things and more.

Marketing is an umbrella term that is used to describe all of the processes that create, communicate, and deliver offerings that have value. Although selling is a process within the marketing institution, marketing is more than just selling goods and services. Marketing is about delivering value and benefits to customers using strategies in communication, pricing, and distribution. Bottom line, marketing creates sales opportunities.

Marketing allows you to provide goods, services, values, benefits, ideas, and information to those who demand it. From the development of your first product/service, to the sale of your offerings, marketing has a function in most aspects of your business. Even the relationships you build with your repeat customers involves marketing. Knowledge of this institution is vital to the success of your business.

Marketing Management Philosophies

The way a company chooses to manage their marketing responsibilities can be widely varied depending on their strengths and weaknesses. Most businesses choose one of three philosophies: Production Orientation, Sales Orientation, or Market Orientation. Each philosophy strongly influences an organization's marketing processes.

A company that focuses on what they can do best and produce the easiest has a production orientation. Companies that concentrate primarily on aggressive sales techniques are sales oriented. These two philosophies can be effective in certain special situations, but they both have a big flaw; they take the focus away from market demand. There is much risk in selling what your company makes rather than what the market wants. If the market doesn't demand our product or service, it doesn't matter how effective you are at producing it nor does it matter how good you are at selling it.

Companies who embrace a market orientation concentrate on fulfilling the needs, wants, and demands of the market first. These companies obtain information about customers, competitors, and markets; examine the information from the total business point-of-view, and determine how to deliver superior value to your customers. You should choose this marketing management philosophy for your company because it places the focus where belongs, on the consumer. Providing the customer with what they want, when they want it will always be a winning combination.

The Marketing Mix

The term marketing mix describes the processes used to create and deliver a product or service to the market. The marketing mix is commonly known as the four P' s: Product, Price, Place, and Promotion. The strategies you develop in each one of these marketing elements on will directly affect the success of your marketing efforts. To achieve the best results, the strategies for all four elements must mix well together to create one cohesive unit. All of the promotion in the world can't save an overpriced, poor product. As well, a great product cannot thrive without effective promotion.

Marketing Mix Elements

Product		Price
Product Variety	Brand Name	List Price
Quality	Packaging	Discounts
Design	Sizes	Allowances
Features	Services	Payment Period
Returns	Warranties	Credit Terms
Promotion		Place (Distribution)
Sales Promotion		Channels
Advertising		Area Coverage
Sales Force		Product Assortment
Public Relations		Locations
Direct Marketing		Inventory
		Warehousing
		Transport
		Logistics

Finding the optimal mix can take some time and effort. You will need to fine-tune your strategies to gain competitive advantages and best serve the needs of your target customers. After developing the product that your customer's demand, you must find the price that will satisfy the market, cover your cost, and leaves enough room for profit. Then, once you figure out the best way to deliver your product to the customer, you need to promote it so that they know it's available. When you find the correct configuration of the marketing mix elements, your product has a great chance to thrive in the market.

Marketing Mix Strategies

Product - Your product offering (which includes services) is the beginning of the marketing mix. It is the core element and your starting point before you can price, place, and promote you need to have a product to market.

Developing your product offering requires some strategic decisions. Before creating the product itself, you must analyze the market to determine what consumers want and are willing to pay for it. A cost-efficient method for producing your product must also be devised. Additionally, your product strategy can include packaging, branding, warranty, after-sale service, guarantees, and other factors. The taste of Coca-Cola is only one component of their product. The unique bottle design, the logos, the color scheme, even the name "Coca-Cola" is all part of their entire product offering.

Price - Since pricing has a direct correlation to revenue, it may be tempting to just charge as much as you can for your product, this may not be the best strategy though. You should consider your costs, how much your customers will pay, and the going rate for similar products (market value), when determining the price of your product.

Pricing can be a powerful competitive weapon. You can price your similar products lower than your competitor's, or you can create a superior product for the same price as your competitor's; both options can offer you a potential advantage. There are several pricing strategies to choose from, but the one that moves the most units and creates the most revenue is the best choice for your company.

Place (Distribution) - Place, or distribution, strategies are about bringing your product to the market. The key is getting your product to customers when and where they want it. You wouldn't travel all the way to South America for Columbian coffee; you want to get it from your local grocery.

When devising place strategies, the main factors to consider are convenience and cost. The goal is to make your product easily accessible to customers by delivering it with cost efficiency. The easier it is to obtain your product the more units you will sell. Lower distribution costs mean lower prices which translates into more units sold. Clearly, place is an important element in the marketing mix.

Promotion - The promotion aspect of the marketing mix is all about communication; getting the word out about your product offering. This includes advertising, public relations, sales promotion, and direct marketing. The point is to inform, persuade, educate, convince, and remind your target customers about the benefits of your product. 'You then want them to know that your product is available, where they can buy, and how they can buy.

Base your promotion strategy on your target customer, the type of product you offer, the area you serve, your available resources, and numerous other variables. Promotion can have a dramatic effect on your sales volume; however, you need to develop adequate strategies in all of the other elements of your marketing mix because good promotion alone won't guarantee sales. A successful promotional strategy builds awareness of your product or brand and attracts lots of potential customers to your business.

Segment the Market

What do you sell? Most likely it's some type of good or service. Let's say, for example, that you sell insurance. The market for insurance is huge because everyone needs it. There are literally billions of people and organizations that need insurance, have the ability to purchase, and are willing to exchange something of value to acquire insurance. This is what makes up a market. A market exists when entities with needs or wants are ready, willing, and able to purchase something they value.

Now let's take this a little bit deeper. Many things can be insured:

Property, vehicles, health, or life, to name a few. You realize that it is not feasible for your fictional insurance company to provide insurance coverage for all of these things; so, you choose to offer simply vehicle insurance. Congratulations you have just segmented the market: You have taken the larger general insurance market. Separated it into segments and specialized in the vehicle insurance portion. If you choose, you can segment the market even further by insuring only automobiles instead of all vehicle types. A market segment is a subgroup of people (or organizations) who have similar characteristics which cause them to have similar product needs.

You are probably thinking: "why would I segment my market?" "Won't a smaller market mean less revenue?" Good questions! The purpose of market segmentation is identification and focus. Identifying a segment of the market with similar characteristics allows you to better focus your marketing mix strategies on the behaviors, needs, and demands of that particular segment. Additionally, segmentation doesn't make the market smaller; it just means that you serve a smaller portion of it. This has the potential to not only enhance the effectiveness of your marketing efforts but actually increase your revenue as a result.

Market segmentation will be an important tool in your marketing arsenal. If utilized correctly, it will help you to navigate a diverse market by giving you a clearer picture of it. Further, because market segments differ in size and potential, segmentation will also help you to define your marketing objectives more accurately and better allocate resources. When you develop more precise objectives, you can better evaluate performance.

To successfully segment a market there are some basic criteria to follow.

A useful segmentation scheme will produce segments that are:

Substantial - There must be enough potential customers in the segment to be worth your time and attention. If you are going to dedicate a special marketing mix to a segment, it must be large enough to make commercial sense.

Identifiable - You must be able to identify members of the segment clearly. They must have some similar relevant characteristics such as age, gender, location, etc.

Measurable - A successful market segment can be measured easily. The most common measures are size and spending power. The number of people in a segment and how much the segment is worth are valuable pieces of information.

Accessible - You need to be able to reach the segment. This sounds simple enough, but some segments are difficult to reach such as foreign language speakers or senior citizens.

Responsive - The segment must be responsive to your marketing mix efforts. If the segment is unresponsive, you may have created the segment incorrectly.

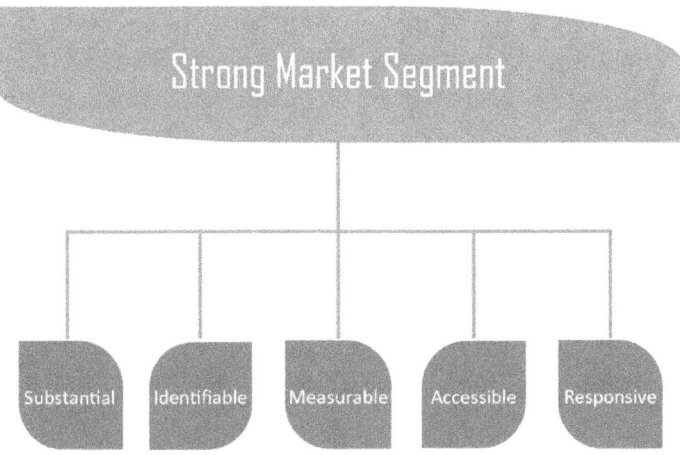

The variables most commonly used to divide a market into segments are geography, demographics, and psychographics.

These are characteristics that people will have in common. You will use these variables to help you identify segments that are substantial, measurable, accessible, and responsive.

Segmenting by geography means to separate based on location, market size, market density, or climate. Different regions, even within the same country, can have vastly different cultures which affect wants and needs. For example, people in New England will eat more clam chowder, while people in Louisiana would prefer crawfish. Note that regions can be of any size you choose, from entire continents, all the way down to a single neighborhood. Also, densely populated areas may merit more marketing attention from your company because of their revenue potential. Climate plays a role in geographical segmentation because of its impact on purchasing behavior. Colder climates will see higher demand on coats and boots, and naturally, warmer climates will demand more shorts and sandals.

Demographics are probably the most popular segmentation base. Information is readily available, and it is directly related to consumer buying behavior. Traditionally, demographic classifications include Age, gender, ethnic background, income, and family life cycle. Demographic information is so effective for segmentation purposes because of the key differences it identifies between people. Usually, marketers mix types to make a more precise segment. "Middle income, Asian, Females, aged 26-34" is an example of a mixed demographic segment.

The demographic variables are very helpful in creating market segmentation strategies, but they don't always tell the entire story.

Psychographic elements work in conjunction with demographics to create a clear picture of a market segment.

The most important psychographic variables include:

Personality: A person's traits, attitudes, habits, and character. Some people like vibrant colored tennis shoes with unique designs, while others prefer a more basic plain type of tennis shoes with a traditional design. Fashion reflects personality which influences preferences.

Lifestyles: How a person lives; how they spend their time. Lifestyle can have a strong influence on buying behavior. World travelers, car enthusiasts, surfers, art buffs, gym rats, and gamers all have different lifestyles; therefore, different demands.

Motives: Why people do things. What motivates them to buy. A father's motive for purchasing life insurance is security for his children in the case of his death. A daughter's motive for purchasing life insurance for her father is to cover funeral costs and final debts.

You can improve the precision of your market segments by mixing bases. Since segmentation bases act as filters, adding more will further eliminate those who may not want, or need your product offering. A segment consisting of simply "White Males in the United States" is not as precise as creating a segment of "White Males, 40 - 60 years old, living in Boulder Colorado, upper income, who enjoy skiing." Make your segments as accurate as possible, but be careful not to over-do it and exclude potential customers.

A strong segmentation strategy will increase the effectiveness of your marketing communications. Knowing the characteristics, nuances, and behaviors of a segment allows you to speak to them more directly. When you create solid segments, you will be able to collect an abundance of information on them. You can then use this information to select targets, tailor your messages, and ultimately sell your products.

Base your promotion strategy will on your target customer, the type of product you offer, the area you serve, your available resources, and numerous other variables. Promotion can have a dramatic effect on your sales volume; however, you need to develop adequate strategies in all of the other elements of your marketing mix because good promotion alone won't guarantee sales. A successful promotional strategy builds awareness of your product or brand and attracts lots of potential customers to your business.

Find Your Target

After dividing the market into identifiable segments, you need to select one or more targets to focus on. A target market is a segment of the market that you have chosen to devote a specific marketing mix to. Choosing a target means to use your marketing resources to meet the unique needs of a group to create mutually beneficial exchanges with them (like selling them your products in exchange for their money). Selecting a target is a crucial marketing decision for your company because it has a direct effect on your success.

When it comes to targeting strategies most companies use one of the following:

Undifferentiated Targeting: mass marketing philosophy with the absence of segmentation. Those who use this strategy don't segment the market at all. They use one marketing mix for the entire market.

Multi-segment Targeting: Developing distinct marketing mixes for two or more segments. Marketing resources are divided to meet the needs of each well—defined segment. This is achieved with different product offerings or variations of the same product.

Concentrated Targeting: Focusing all marketing efforts on a market niche (single segment). It requires you to develop an intimate understanding of the target to serve their needs directly. Obtaining specific knowledge of a single segment like this allows more effective communication with them.

One-to-one Marketing: Individualized marketing. Seeking out customer one by one and building long-term personalized relationships. The point is to sell more to each customer, build loyalty, and focus on retention. This method is more about quality than quantity.

When determining which targeting strategy to utilize, consider the type of business you are in and what product(s) you sell. For example, if you are the only convenience store in a small town, you may want to use an *undifferentiated* targeting strategy because there is little competition, serve the entire community (market) in general. On the other hand, if you operate an organic food store in an area saturated with grocery stores, dividing the market with a *multi-segment* or *concentrated* targeting strategy would be your best choice because you offer specialized products to one or more segments. Plus, with a multi-segment or concentrated targeting strategy, you may be able to gain an advantage in a particular segment; which will increase your competitiveness. *One-to-one* marketing is best utilized with products that are more expensive and exclusive because often they require customization and more personalized customer service. Each method has its own strengths and weaknesses.

Targeting is all about finding advantages and maximizing your marketing resources. Usually, your product offering will not fulfill the needs of the entire market. As much as you would probably like to, you won't to be able to sell your offering to everyone. But the same is true for your competitors. You will have advantages in certain segments though. That's why it is important for you to not only figure out who needs your product, but who is most willing to buy your product. This is your target. This is where you need to focus! Don't waste time and resources on people who probably won't buy anyway.

When you find your target(s), you will be able to design marketing mixes specifically for them. You will know what products they want, what price they are willing to pay, where they want to buy it from, and how to communicate with them most effectively. Connecting with a segment so intimately can turn prospects into paying customers. Bottom line, a superior targeting strategy will boost your earnings potential.

In military warfare, divide and conquer has always been a solid strategy. The same is true for market share. You divide the market with segmentation, then conquer it with accurate targeting.

Positioned for Success

How do people view your product, brand, or organization as compared to the competition? Is your product seen as lower priced for value, or higher priced with superior quality? Is your brand known as prestigious, or stylish, or reliable? Does your company have a reputation for being charitable or environmentally conscious? These are all examples of positions. The way that potential customers perceive your company and your offering is your market position. Positioning is developing specific marketing mixes to influence these perceptions.

The goal of most positioning strategies is to create differentiation. Usually, you want to separate yourself from the competition as much as possible. This is what makes your company or product stand out in the minds of consumers. Differentiation births preference and lead to customer loyalty. The Jeep brand, for example, is known for their rugged and reliable vehicles. Their customers prefer their brand for this reason. Some will purchase only Jeep brand vehicles as long as they live.

In some instances, alignment, not differentiation, is the positioning goal. Companies will position themselves near the competition to piggyback off of their success. For example, you may want your customers to believe that your less expensive product is comparable in quality to the more popular competitor's product. In this case, you have positioned yourself in line with the competition regarding quality, but you have also created separation, regarding price.

An effective positioning strategy will have several layers. A broad position as the core, and one or more specific positions as the outer layers. You need to establish the broad position as a foundation, and then use the specific position(s) to express more concrete benefits and give consumers a reason to purchase. Using a multi-level system like this helps you to find an overall position in the market that is unique, but also relevant to potential customers.

There are three standard **broad positions**: product differentiation, cost leader, or niche server. Your company should only focus on mastering one of these three broad positions. Product differentiators look to create key differences, no matter how subtle, in their products to stand out from the competition. Low-cost leaders focus on offering their customers the lowest prices all the time. Niche servers direct all of their attention to best serving the needs of a particular segment. Don't try to be in all three positions at once because each requires a different organization, management system, and company culture.

After adopting a broad position, you need to establish a more specific position. This is how you solidify your product's image in the mind of your customers.

The most common bases used to build a specific position include:

Attribute: Focus on features and attributes that are associated with a product. Emphasizing the benefits of using a product.

Use/Application: Emphasis on the uses or applications of a product. Could mean being positioned as the best in a certain application.

Price and Quality: Stressing to customers that higher price is an indication of better quality, or that lower price is a signal of value.

User: Focus on the personality type of the target user group.

Competitor: Suggesting a key difference or superiority from a competitor s product.

Product Class: Associating the product with a particular category of products. Possibly positioning the product as the leader in a category.

Emotion: Positioning based on the feeling that customers get from the use of the product.

In certain cases, after securing a position, you may have to rescind and reposition. This happens when you realize that you have made a positioning mistake, or when new opportunities become available that require you to reposition to capitalize. Developing a position takes an exceptional amount of time, effort, and resources. Repositioning takes even more effort because you must remove yourself from one position to take another. For this reason, you should thoroughly consider any decision to reposition your product, brand, or company.

A strong market position will make your product offering stand out to consumers. No matter what combination of broad and specific positions you adopt, they must appeal to your target customers. If you want them to prefer your brand, love your company, and buy your products, you have to offer them a set of benefits and features that they care about. Then you can use communication to solidify your position, and integrity (being who and what you say you are) to sustain it.

Consumer vs. Business-to-Business Marketing

The target customers of most businesses will be either the everyday consumer or another business. Marketing your products to businesses requires a different approach than marketing them to consumers. This is because there are some key characteristic contrasts between the customer types. Their purchasing behaviors, influences, purchase volume, and product utilization are all different.

Everyday consumers are a diverse group of billions with varying purchasing behaviors. Some are brand aware and very loyal, while others have no loyalty and care only about the best price. Depending on the type of product, consumer buying decisions can range from loose and impulsive, to strict and very involved. The influences of consumer purchasing behavior include Culture, values, social class, lifestyle, perception, and beliefs. Consumers purchase their goods and services in low volumes and use them for personal consumption.

Marketing to consumers is largely about image and perception. You are what people perceive you to be. Fortunately, consumers are easier to reach, persuade and influence than business customers. Constant and consistent communication is the key. You will need to spend marketing dollars to make consumers aware of the value and benefits of your product offering, but most times, it is enough to convince them to buy. If they give your product a chance, you then build trust and loyalty by delivering on your promises.

Business customers are a smaller group in number but have significantly larger spending power. Businesses usually designate a buyer to make their purchases. Professional buyers are more concerned with price and quality than brand names. They are very involved and meticulous with their buying decisions. They will take the time to do research and compare options in order to make the best choice. Professional buyers are only influenced by the department heads, within their company, for whom they may be buying. Businesses are high volume purchasers. A single customer, like Ford Motor Company, can account for huge orders worth billions per year in revenue.

Business-to-business marketing requires persistence and finesse. Access to business customers can be severely limited making them harder to communicate with and persuade. Professional buyers tend to be more careful and considerate when making their purchasing decisions. Remember, they are potentially spending thousands of company dollars with each purchase, so on-thesurface marketing will not be enough to convince them to buy. Broad communication efforts can open the door, but patient personal selling will close the deal.

Business customers want mutually beneficial, close relationships with their suppliers. They look for someone who will consistently have the materials or products they need (on demand), so they can conduct their business uninterrupted. You must be willing to make several sales call visits, customize your product to their specifications, negotiate price, offer discounts, and provide post-purchase support. This way, you can show them that not only are your products dependable but so are you.

There are some universal principles to follow when marketing your products to either businesses or consumers:

Know your target. Learn everything you can about them. The more you understand your target, the better you can serve their needs.

Establish effective communications with your target. Figure out how to speak to directly. Tell them how you will fulfill their needs. Overcome their objections.

Express the value of your product. What is it about your product that you want your target to value? Make sure that they understand that your product is worth every penny that you are asking them to pay for it.

Maintain Integrity. Make sure that your product does what is says that it will do. Be trustworthy and reliable as a company.

Marketing Goods vs. Marketing Services

You've finally saved up enough for the down payment on that new car you have been wanting. You've dreamed of this day for a long time. As you arrive at the dealership, you get a glimpse of its shiny new excellence. You can't wait to get in and drive it off the lot.

Noticing the excited look in your eyes, a salesperson rushes over to assist you with your purchase. After intense negotiations, you and the dealer agree on a fair price. In addition to the vehicle, the salesperson persuades you to buy the bigger upgraded rims, a satellite radio subscription, and an extended warranty. You are satisfied with the deal, and you seal it by signing a finance agreement with the bank. Now you are riding in style. The car of your dreams has become a reality!

The purchase you just made includes a combination of goods and services. The vehicle and the rims are **goods**; tangible products also known as merchandise. The satellite radio subscription, the extended warranty, and the financing are all **services**; intangible products, Fundamentally, goods and services are different types of products; therefore, each requires a unique marketing mix strategy.

Product strategy (the first "P" of the marketing mix elements) for goods includes: Drafting, prototyping, extensive testing, and finally manufacturing. Inventing an entirely new product can be difficult though. This is why most new product development is limited to variation, modification, and/or improvement of products that are already in existence. Also, you must consider packaging, labeling, branding, and product lines when developing a goods product.

On the other hand, product development strategy for services is about designing a unique process or series of processes. The object is to create a combination of core and supplementary services that will offer solutions to your customer's problems. Service products should be flexible with a higher level of customization ability to adequately fit customer needs. The trick is finding the things that people can't do themselves, or don't want to do themselves, and offer to do it for them as a service. Depending on your strategy, determining the price of a goods product is generally easier than pricing a service. In its simplest form, pricing a goods product is based on first covering costs to break even, then adding a markup for profit. Your per unit overhead cost is made up of all your fixed costs, plus all your variable costs, divided by the number of units produced. Add your markup amount, and you have your selling price.

Now, this is only a simple example. Your pricing strategy can be as complex a calculation as you choose. Either way, you will have more concrete figures to work with when pricing goods because you will know exactly how many units you can produce at a specific cost.

The intangible nature of service products makes them slightly more complicated to price. You must first determine what a unit of consumption is for your service. Is it based on completion of a task (flat rate), or the time it takes to complete that task (hourly rate)? Once you decide what makes a unit, you need to calculate the costs associated with providing this unit of service. Since many of these costs are variable costs, it may prove to be a challenge tracking them adequately. Be prepared for some trial and error the final price of your service product. Your bottom-line objective should be to offer value while making profits.

Placing, or distributing, goods to the market means to deliver them to the consumer physically. This requires you to set up a marketing channel and a corresponding supply chain. A marketing channel is a business structure of interdependent organizations that help to bring a product from the producer to the consumer. The organizations within the channel work together to support the logistics function, creating the supply chain. The chain can be of varying lengths and can include intermediaries like brokers, wholesalers, and retailers who will cooperate to distribute goods to consumers. The best distribution strategies will get your products in the right place at the time making them readily available for purchase.

The main factor in distributing service products is convenience. You want to make it as easy as possible for customers to use your service. This could mean having several locations, in-home delivery, 24/7 availability, internet distribution, or flexible scheduling. Today's consumer expects their services to be on demand. You can accommodate them by offering the conveniences they want.

To promote any product, you must build awareness, sell benefits, and express value. Make people aware of the benefits of your product, and they will begin to develop a value for it. Communicate your message effectively, and ultimately people will buy. Goods products have physical attributes; they may look a certain way or have unique features. The tangible qualities of goods are easily translated into desirable benefits; therefore, promoting them is less difficult.

Service products have intangible attributes, so promotion can be complicated. Since consumers have problems evaluating services, communicating benefits and expressing value can give you some trouble. There are a few ways that you can improve your success though. First, stress tangible cues (symbols of your product offering). Tangible cues give consumers something concrete to identify your product with. Also, use real people to speak for your service. It needs to be someone that people trust and can relate to like a celebrity spokesperson or current satisfied customers. Finally, build a strong organizational image. For example, maintain the physical ascetics of your business premises, and/or keep the appearance of your employees consistent. Create uniformity among all the visual aspects of your service. All of these promotional strategies will help you to transform intangible attributes into tangible benefits that consumers recognize and appreciate.

As you can see, the same marketing mix strategies you use for goods won't necessarily work for services. Each requires a distinct approach. Understanding this will help you to choose the most effective strategies for your particular product. Goods are physically created, have a precise value, are made available to consumers using logistical measures, and can be promoted based on well-defined attributes. Service products are processes specifically designed to solve certain problems, their value is based upon obscure variables, they are distributed using locations that maximize convenience and accessibility, and promoting them is about communicating tangible benefits and shaping perceptions.

There are common objectives for marketing any product to any customer. First, create a product that the market demands. Next, find the optimal price that the market will pay while optimizing your profits. Then, make your product conveniently available to the market. Finally, build awareness of your product and persuade the market to buy. These are the principles that will deliver value and benefits to customers. The end result is mutually satisfying exchanges.

∞

Now that you have a basic understanding of the marketing fundamentals, you can begin developing your marketing plan. Don't worry; it's easier than you think. You'll be surprised. Just turn the page, and you can get started right away!

Chapter 3:
The Do-it-Yourself
Marketing Plan

It should be apparent now that developing a marketing plan is crucial to the success of your business. But can you complete something this important on your own? The answer. emphatically yes! If you have the time to invest, you can create a strategic marketing plan that will put your business on the path to prosperity.

Before you can begin writing your own plan, you must do some priming. This chapter will help you to get prepared.

What Your Marketing Consultant Doesn't Want You to Know

Up to $150 per hour-potentially thousands per project. This is what a marketing consultant will charge you to help with your marketing plans. Your consultant will conduct research, analyze the findings, and devise strategies to best take advantage of your perceived opportunities. Completing the plan will take the consultant anywhere from a few days up to a month depending on the depth and complexity of it.

Your marketing consultant will be a consummate professional-- She will be knowledgeable and experienced. The plan she submits will be thoroughly written. It will be a roadmap for your company to follow. So, what is it that your marketing consultant doesn't want you to know? It's all still just a guess. What's more, you can do it too!

All of the strategies devised from a marketing plan are simply guesses. You guess what strategy will work best based upon the information you collect. The higher quality your information is, the more accurate your guesses will be. The better you analyze the information, the more precise your strategy will be.

The point is, marketing consultants make educated guesses, and you can do the same, with the right tools. All you need to know is what information to look for, and then how to use it. When you finish this manual, you'll understand both.

Collecting the Right Information

To complete a marketing plan, you need to gather information about the history of your business, your competitors and their businesses, the industry you are in, your target customers, and many other aspects. This data will be the basis of your planning efforts. Since we are currently in the middle of an "information age," information is easy to get because it is abundant and readily available. Don't be fooled though; there's a large amount of "noise" (invalid or irrelevant information) out there that can get in your way as well. Avoiding the noise and choosing the best information requires some filtering.

Where do you get your information from? Information gathering begins with sources. There are two types of information: primary and secondary. Primary information is collected straight from the source interviews, surveys, experiments, or inquiries. Secondary information comes from other sources that have collected data and processed it their way (books, news, magazines, reports, etcetera.).

Reliable sources provide the best information. Primary sources are generally reliable because you are collecting the information yourself. This way, the reliability depends on your effort and accuracy. If you surveyed the smells that homemakers prefer in their laundry detergents, this would be a great primary source of customer information. Likewise, conducting a test with different price points for the laundry detergent would yield important pricing information. Although it requires more work, primary sources are your most credible sources of information.

That doesn't mean that secondary sources are completely fallacious. There are various secondary sources that can be reliable, you just have to know where to look. When searching online, for instance, you can rely on sites whose domain name ends in a ".gov" or ".org." You can trust the statistics that you gather from census.gov (US Census Bureau), or amstat.org (American Statistics Organization) because these are well-known and trustworthy entities. The information that governments and organizations release is universally considered to be accurate and solid.

You will know a reliable secondary source when you see it. You have probably heard of the author and the organization s/he represents, the work will appear professional, and various credible sources will be cited within the work. If you aren't sure about it, don't use it!

You should also consider the age of the information you are collecting. Older information is more likely to be outdated. New information comes out all the time that can contradict or supplement older data. To maximize the accuracy of your information, be sure to use only the most current and vetted information that you can find.

The last thing that you want is to fill out your marketing plan with data that is later found to be unreliable, outdated, and inaccurate. As the old saying goes: "anything worth doing is worth doing right." Invest the time and effort into collecting quality information and your marketing plan will be a highly effective document for your company.

<u>Turning Data into Knowledge</u>

What is the difference between data and knowledge? Data is just raw information--facts, figures, statistics, and evidence. Knowledge is data that has been processed and interpreted into meaning. You can gain knowledge by compiling several bits of analogous data and drawing conclusions. Knowledge is understanding.

If you want to convert data into knowledge, you need to know how each piece applies to your inquiry. For instance; you know that Product A has sold 700,000 units, and your inquiry pertains to finding market trends. This information can be used as a base. Even though 700,000 units seems significant, you need to know what the comparison is? You must establish a point of reference and context.

To conduct a full analyzation, you will need to collect additional corresponding data to cross-reference.

If "Product A" sold 700,000 units, ask:

- In what time frame were these units sold?
- What were the previous sales in the same timeframe?
- Are the sales concentrated in a single area, several smaller areas, or spread out over a large area?
- Can supply keep up with demand, or is there a shortage?
- Has the customer base expanded or remained homeostatic?
- Have additional resources been devoted to communication recently?

These are just a few of the questions that will provide supplementary facts and evidence giving you a view of the subject. If you decide that a trend exist, you can use this knowledge to devise a strategy to capitalize on this trend.

Obtaining knowledge is like drawing a picture. Adding more layers and details make the picture clearer. Let's say, for example, that you want to build knowledge of the competition in your particular market. Many pieces of data are needed to achieve this objective. The more information you collect about the competition, the better you will understand them. A single fact, like the number of competitors in the market, is good information, but not adequate alone for a complete understanding. To get a real view of the competition, you need to know their history, their share of the market, their sales, their product line, etcetera.

Any intelligence you gather can be valuable, but you must know how to use it. For facts, evidence, and figures to mean something they have to be collaborated together and analyzed correctly. This is how you condense facts into knowledge.

Organize Your Findings

Magnenarter...What does this mean? Absolutely nothing. Right now, this is just ten letters assembled in no particular order; but organize them differently, and they spell **arrangement**. Information is meaningless until it is organized and arranged.

This manual provides you with a blueprint on how to organize your data. You will use the most important marketing aspects to categorize and make sense of the information you collect. Each category has key questions that show you what information to look for, then makes it easy to interpret. After completing a section, you will use the knowledge gained to devise strategies to capitalize on your opportunities.

You will organize your findings using the following categories:

- Company History

- Market Analysis

- Competition

- Marketing Mix

- Communications

- Sales

- Financial Plan

All of these components blend to create a comprehensive outlook. Categorizing your information this way gives you a unique insight into your business. This is how you gain a deeper understanding of the market and where your company fits in it.

Strategic Management

The whole point of creating a marketing plan is to develop strategies that help you meet your marketing objectives and sell your product offering. Strategic decisions determine the course your business will take to achieve your goals and how your resources will be allocated. The way you execute your everyday business operations will be based directly on your strategy. If you are meticulous and thorough in your planning, your strategies will be superior.

The marketing plan is your playbook, use it to make the strategic decisions that will lead your company to success. As you complete each section, the challenges you must face will be revealed. The information you collect helps you to choose the best solutions. Each of the key components included in your marketing plan will have a corresponding strategy that specifically details your approach to that component. Your strategies should work together to satisfy your organizational goals and promote overall growth. Your strategic theme will need to focus on taking advantage of opportunities in the market. Ansoff's strategic opportunity matrix is a model that helps you discover market opportunities. The matrix is a method for matching products with markets.

There are four options that you can explore:

- **Market Penetration:** Increasing market share among your existing customers. This strategy is executed with additional direct communications (advertising, promotions, etcetera) with current customers in an attempt to persuade them to buy more of your products. Example: A campaign where your customer's database is used to send all of your existing customers coupons, offering discounts on your products. Alternatively, a sweepstakes sales promotion that offers a grand prize to a customer who has the winning number on their product's packaging.

- **Market Development:** Attracting new customers to your existing products. Emphasizing new uses and different benefits is an effective way to attract new customers. Example: When all-terrain vehicles were introduced to the public, they were marketed as tools for work. Communicating the recreational uses of these vehicles has drawn an entirely new type of customer to these products.

- **Product Development:** Creation of new products for markets already in existence. Basically, develop new offerings for the same customers. Example: Creating boneless chicken tenders and offering them to customers in the traditional (bone-in) chicken market.

- **Diversification:** Increasing sales by introducing new products in new markets. Entering an unfamiliar market can be very risky, but if you can create a desirable product, the market will be wide open w with little or no competition. Example: Diversify your salon business by introducing your own line of haircare products, cosmetics, robes, and fragrances for sale.

Ansoff's Strategic Opportunity Matrix

	Existing	New
New Markets	**Market Development** New market with an existing product:	**Diversification** New market with a new product:
Existing	**Market Penetration** Existing market with an existing product:	**Product Development** Existing market with a new product:

Existing   Products and Services   New

Don't be too nervous when choosing your strategies because they aren't set in stone. Market planning s an ongoing process. Don't think of it as a one—time chore. It is helpful to think of your marketing plan as a "living document." It must be flexible and evolve as your organizational needs evolve. You will have to update your marketing plan, and its strategies, frequently to adapt to the ever-changing—sometimes volatile—market environment.

You don't have to be a strategic genius to create effective strategies. Your organizational marketing objectives will provide you with a destination to reach. As you get further into your planning, your course of action will become clear. You just need to be patient, persistent, and unafraid to fail. Remember, failures are assets; they will provide you with the best information of all.

Use Your Imagination

That time you spent in creative writing class is about to pay off. Not for the writing styles, but for the improved ability to utilize your imagination. Creating innovative strategies to meet your marketing objectives requires a certain level of ingenuity. Your imagination will be invaluable to this end.

The phrase "think outside the box" is grossly overused, but it best describes what you need to do in your market planning efforts. When you are brainstorming new ideas, no idea is too crazy. Every idea should be considered. Some may seem far-fetched, but you will come across others that are truly brilliant. To find these gems, you must be open-minded and unrestricted in your thinking. Not to suggest that you totally disregard conventional marketing concepts. Tried and true methods can be highly effective towards achieving your desired outcome. Just don't let conventional thinking limit your imaginative thinking. Your riskier, more unorthodox ideas should be supplementary to your safer, more plain ideas. This way your marketing plan has stability, but also creativity.

The secret to staying ahead of the competition is thinking on a different plane. You need to go where they won't go, do what they won't do, develop your own unique identity, and create your signature. If you operate, for example, in a drab, boring, and highly technical industry, find a new way to make light of it. Draw up a marketing campaign that takes a normally serious topic (like insurance, financial instruments, computer software, or manufacturing) and portray it in a lighthearted and funny way. Companies like Geico, Intel, e-trade, and GoDaddy.com are famous for this.

When you utilize marketing techniques that are new, fresh, and original you will stand out in the minds of consumers and make a splash in the market. If you want to discover important competitive advantages, be pragmatic but imaginative in your marketing planning.

∞

At this point, you are well-prepared to take on the task of writing your own marketing plan. You know what information to look for, how to organize it, and how to use it to build effective marketing strategies. Let's move forward and finally explore the components of a formal marketing plan. That Is the whole reason you bought this manual right?☐

Section Two:

Creating your Marketing Plan

Overview:

The most successful businesses carefully plan their marketing activities. Market planning is your roadmap to prosperity. The better your planning the clearer your path will be. However, a roadmap isn't useful until you put it on paper. All the intangible thoughts, ideas, and concepts of your marketing department must be compiled into a tangible, written, measurable plan. That is what this section is all about, the formal marketing plan.

The following chapters will break down all of the components of a marketing plan. You will learn exactly what information you need to include in your own plan to ensure that it's thorough and effective. You will discover how the individual parts of your marketing plan will come together to form a cohesive document that coordinates all your marketing initiatives. Most importantly, you will see that good planning has a direct effect on the success of your business.

Your marketing plan will begin with a description of your organization and a complete analysis of your market. From there, you'll review the marketing mix elements (product, price, and place only) as they pertain to your operation. Then, you will learn how to define and develop your communication strategy. Profiling your competition and building a sales plan are discussed next. Finally, Chapter 11 covers cash flow statements and budgets.

As you can see, we have much to go over. So, let's jump right in.

Chapter 4:
Marketing Plan Part One
Company Description

Writing the marketing plan is like charting the course on your path to prosperity. You want to find the shortcuts, note the obstacles, and plot your previous movements. Keep adding quality information, and before you know it, you will have a well-detailed roadmap.

Your first task in writing a marketing plan is profiling your company. Those making the marketing decisions within your organization need a complete understanding of the company identity to adhere to it. Before any marketing protocols, procedures, and initiatives can be set you must have an exact knowledge of the company interests. This chapter will show you how to create a profile of your organization based on its history, current state, and projected future.

History

"The past is the best predictor of the future." "History always repeats itself. "You got to know where you been to know where you're going." Any cliché about past, present, and future will fit here. The point is, your company history is a key component in developing your organization's profile.

A thorough examination of your company history will break down your business into its most basic elements. Take a look at who your company is, where it has come from, and what it stands for. These are the roots from which your company grows. If you want continuous healthy growth, you must acknowledge and understand your roots. You will find that analyzing the history of your company will be beneficial in a variety of ways.

When it comes to the marketing plan, your company's historical data plays a major role. It's used to establish the foundation of principles and values that are important to your organization. You will utilize these philosophical standards as a basis for setting the objectives that will guide your marketing plan. Developing clear objectives from your organizational principles helps to keep you focused and ensures that your marketing efforts stay on track. Also, the company history section of the marketing plan provides benchmarks that can be used to gauge progress. Knowing what you have already tried, tested, and accomplished allows you to determine if you are moving forward or backward with your marketing efforts.

How You Got Started

The story of how your company got started contains fundamental historical data. Questions like when you were founded, where you were founded, and who is the founder, begins to build an identity for the company. Recall your original mission and the philosophy that your company was founded upon, to establish this identity further. Maintaining organizational integrity is about staying true to your fundamental values. This is why customers will trust you, and employees will respect you. Always acknowledge the origin of your enterprise.

Corporate Values

Your corporate values are one of the most important aspects of your company's history. Corporate values are the things your company believes in, the tenants that it stands for, and what is uniquely important to it. Your values may include honesty, integrity, fairness, and family. These are the principles that guide your life. Corporate values are the principles that govern your company.

Enduring organizations understand that corporate values transcend strategic objectives. Any strategy that is contradictory to your company's value system should be discarded and replaced with an alternative. Never sacrifice potential longevity for short-term success. Staying adhered to your core ideologies is the only way to reach your envisioned future. Remember why you got into business in the first place.

The Purpose You Serve

What was your company's original purpose? What did you set out to accomplish? What problem did you solve, or need did you satisfy? These questions will provide you with relevant pieces of information about the DNA of your organization. You must understand your original purpose to know if you have been headed in the right direction so far.

Previous Marketing Strategies

The marketing strategies you've utilized in the past should be noted in your marketing plan as well. Excellent learning opportunities come from the successes or failures of the different strategies that your company may have used before. You extract these valuable lessons by evaluating your previous strategies to determine why certain ones worked and why others didn't. You can avoid making crucial mistakes in future judgment by reviewing your previous marketing strategies.

Other Historical Facts

Be sure to include any other information about the history of your business that you feel is appropriate. This could mean company traditions, corporate structures, past major events, PR occurrences, philanthropic efforts/obligations, business affiliations, or anything else that may have marketing implications. The more information, the better. You can never have too much. Your objective? Paint the most accurate picture of your organization possible.

The Organization Today

Now that you have realized your company's past identity; you can begin looking at what your company is currently. This is the next step in developing your profile. As you continue to dissect and study your organization you should think about how it has changed over time, the type of company it has become, the image it maintains, and the business model it employs.

How Your Company Has Changed

Businesses constantly evolve (or they should anyway) to match evolving markets, it's only natural. Preferences change, environments change, economies fluctuate, and technology gets upgraded. To keep up with all these extenuating circumstances, your company must adapt and change right along with them. Changes your company has made regarding the mission, operations, management, location, or product/service offering should be documented in your marketing plan to show progression.

Company Types

The next part of the profile is about categorizing your company. In other words, what type of company are you? Is your focus on innovation or efficient operations? Are you service oriented, or price-oriented? Are you old-fashioned, or progressive? What is the culture of your organization? All of your company's unique characteristics should be listed here. These are the traits that you will want to exploit and highlight in your marketing plan.

Don't stop there though. Think about the physical characteristics of your company as well. For example, do you operate a "brick-and-mortar" location, an internet storefront, or both? Each platform has different needs when it comes to marketing and promotions, so it is important to note which you are operating. Other noteworthy physical traits of your organization include size, age, number of employees, corporate hierarchy, trademarks (color combinations, logos, wordings, others), patients, copyrights, financial standing, and tax status.

What about your employees? Are they highly trained? Do they have unique professional experience? Are they known for their world-class courtesy? Having special employees makes your company special as well and is worthy of being regarded in your profile.

Company Image

They say image is everything. Whoever "they" are is exactly right. Company image is derived in many different ways and crucial to your business. Everything that your company does is a part of its image. The way you sell your products/services, the way you operate your organization, the way you treat your employees, the way you treat your customers, the causes you believe in, the charitable work you do, almost every aspect of your business build image. For this reason, you should first calculate and carefully consider every move you make.

The public is always watching, criticizing, and building their perception of who you are (as a company). Regardless of how you feel, in business, you are what people perceive you to be. Always remember that. It doesn't matter that your company may actually be different than the public thinks it is. In this case, you must shape their perceptions (through PR and advertising) until they see you favorably. Your job, as a business owner, is to ensure that your company's image matches your company's true identity.

So, how does all of this pertain to the marketing plan? Primarily because all marketing activities must be consistent with the image you've chosen to portray. If you want to maintain or possibly enhance your company image, you must first be conscious of it. Establish this in the marketing plan by simply describing your company as you see it. Then consider the description that you feel your customers would give. Would they use the same adjectives you used?

Take this a step further by actually asking your customers how they view your business. Be sure to record their answers so you can compare and contrast your description with their description. Once you identify the gap between public perception and your desired company image you can strategically plan the marketing activities that will fill the gap.

Business Model

A company profile cannot be considered as complete without reviewing your business model. The term business model refers to the unique way your business is structured and operated. Everything you do to satisfy the needs of a chosen market is a part of your business model. For the purposes of the marketing plan though, we will focus on the "soft" aspects such as business mission, the product/service you offer, the problem your offering solves, your operational procedures, and how you achieve differentiation.

Business Mission

There's a reason why you started your business in the first place. You had an ultimate vision of changing the world in some way with your business idea. There was something you wanted to achieve, something you set out to accomplish. This is your chosen mission, and it is the heart of your business model.

Articulate your business mission in the form of a mission statement. A meaningful statement inspires the people inside your company, is deliberately broad so that potential is limitless, expresses a position that will remain valid for years to come, and is truly reflective of what your company is all about. Your mission statement is the basis of your business model.

The Product You Offer

Fully describe the product (service) you sell as a part of your business model. How it's made, the raw materials used to make it, who makes it, the quality of it, the price its sold for, the profit margin that is made on it, and any of the other traits you feel should be included.

The Problem You Solve/Need you Fulfill

After detailing your product, specify the problem it solves and the need it fulfills. Products and services only exist as solutions. The better you can understand the issues that your offering accommodates, the better you can express the value of it to your customers.

Whenever you find an unsolved problem, there is also a need to be satisfied. Don't think of needs strictly in the sense of "can't live without." From a marketing standpoint, if they don't already have it, then they need it. The only question is how to convince you, (the consumer) of that.

Of course, those things that are actual needs (food, clothing, shelter, medical assistance) don't take as much persuading, but any product can be perceived as a need. Creative marketing can turn people's wants into needs. You want that new juicer because you like to try different and exotic drinks. Marketers convince you that you need this juicer because of the health benefits, money savings, and the overall good feeling you'll get from owning it. In this example, the product solves the problem of inefficient juicing options and fulfills the need for healthy drink alternatives.

What is the need that your product/ service satisfies? What is the problem it solves? Answer these questions in your company profile to offer some additional insight into your business model.

Your System of Operation

As a small business owner, you may run your business mostly on your own. You probably do all the primary work creating your product (or delivering your service), only entrusting others to do supplementary tasks. However, you can only do so much work yourself. What happens when demand for your product increases beyond your capacity? Will you turn paying customers away? If you don't mind hard work with limited potential, then this is acceptable. Otherwise, you need to develop a system of operation.

The best systems operate the same way no matter whose administering it. This means that others can learn to do all the functions of your business without sacrificing efficiency or quality. It would be just like you had done it yourself. Enter a McDonald's franchise in Santa Monica, California; then visit a McDonalds in Tallahassee, Florida; and you will see several similarities. The drive-thru window and the fryers will always be located to the left, the shake machine will always be on your right, your fries will always taste the same, your Big Mac will always come on a sesame seed bun. The McDonalds system will perform the way you expect it to every time. This directly contributes to their phenomenal success around the world.

Your system of operation is the brains of your business model. It can include the way you make your product (recipe, procedure, etc.), a specific facility layout, a special form of delivery, or anything else that makes your business run uniquely. Whether your system is simple or complex, it needs to be easily duplicated and independent.

If you already have a system in place, record the particulars of it in your marketing plan. This information can be used later for strategy building. If you don't currently have a system, just explain the way you normally operate your business on a daily basis. Begin with the creation of the product/service and end with the final sale. You may be surprised to find out that you already have a system in place, but you just didn't know it.

Differentiation

Attempting to stand out in a competitive market is one of the main challenges of marketing. Creating separation between your company and the competition is absolutely necessary though. In this portion of the marketing plan, you will explain how your company is different and what makes your product offering unique.

It is important to mention that different doesn't always mean better. You don't have to prove superiority to show contrast. If you are superior in some way (price, quality, size, etc.) then, by all means, use that. But remember that differentiation can be achieved just as well with a lateral move based on characteristics like style, taste (food items), function, packaging, coloring, or usage. The point is to build preference for your company or your brand.

Think about all of the qualities that make your enterprise and offering different from your competitors. No matter how insignificant a quality may seem, include it anyway. Every inch of separation counts. This analysis will complete the probe of your company's current status.

Projected Future

Sorry magic 8-ball, your services aren't needed here. In business, the future is projected not predicted. It's less about destiny and more about strategy. The lessons you learned earlier about objectives and goals (see chapter one) will prove useful now. These are the tools that you will use to project the future of your business operation.

In this section of the marketing plan, you will create objectives and set goals for the following categories:

- Market Position
- Sales Revenue
- Profits
- Market Share
- Product Mix

To work towards the future you desire, be proactive and create strong benchmarks here. This is how you take control of your company's destiny instead of waiting to get lucky.

Start by determining a single objective for each category. Remember, objectives are broader by nature, and should always move your company towards achieving overall success.

Don't spend too much time trying to figure this out though. You can be general and simplistic here. Just ask yourself what do you want to accomplish? What will propel your operation in the right direction? Be sure that the objectives you chose in any category are strongly based on your business mission.

Once the objectives are known, you can set the goals that will help you achieve them. Each goal is like a rung on a ladder. Every time you reach one, you climb higher up ascending towards your objective.

Goal setting focuses on the specifics. Goals are the quantifiable measures that you will use to help you plan your business actions. The more precise they are, the more accountability they provide. Later in your business analysis, you can pinpoint strong areas and identify potential problems by reviewing which goals are met and which you may have fallen short on. Then, make adjustments accordingly.

Use hard data and facts to set realistic, attainable goals. The longer you have been in business, the more information you will have at your disposal. Your records should include facts like average sales amounts, sales revenues, number of customers, conversion rate, response rates, profit/earnings ratio, operating costs, and other important data points. These statistics will provide you with a solid control that can be used to keep your goals in check.

It is easy to get overly ambitious and create goals that are too pretentious. The trick is to set the bar at a level that's high enough to yield progress, but yet remain reachable. You can't expect to go too far, too quickly from where you are currently. For instance, if your company has had average revenues of $70,000 per year for the last three years, it is unrealistic to set a goal to make $700,000 in year four (unless you expect a very unusual event in this way) A more appropriate goal would be $100,000 within the next two years.

Example:

Objective – Establish and maintain a broad position as a niche server with a specific focus on high quality exclusive products.

Short-Terms Goals:

- Develop a system of quality control that ensures consistency of product quality.
- Build workforce of highly skilled customer service professionals by hiring new employees and training existing ones.
- Find a premium price point that reflects the exclusivity of the product.
- Create and launch a marketing campaign that communicates our position.

Long-Terms Goals:

- Develop a customer survey system to assess service quality.

- Create a service oriented company culture.

- Build relationships with various suppliers of the highest quality raw materials.

- Affiliate with a single manufacturer that reciprocates our quality standards.

When writing your goals, separate them into long-term and short-term distinctions. Long-term goals are those which you hope to achieve in the next three to five years. Short-term goals are intended to be completed within three years. Making your goals time specific adds another element of accountability. It requires you to maintain a deadline that keeps you prompt and focused. Also, time-sensitive goals are easier to measure because once you reach the deadline, you've either met your goals or you haven't.

As your goal setting skills improve your projections will become more accurate. This is a key business strategy because it promotes growth. It's impossible to remain stagnant when you are accomplishing ever-escalating goals. As you strive and ultimately succeed in achieving them, your business will naturally grow the way you planned. If objectives represent the big red X on your roadmap, then your goals are the checkpoints directing you along the way to your destination.

Market Positioning

What is your desired position? We examined positioning in Chapter 2: "Marketing 101". There, we concluded that positioning is a process that influences the perceptions that consumers have of a brand, product line, or organization. More specifically, a position is the place that a product offering, brand, or group of products holds in the minds of consumers as compared to the competitors.

When you are deciding your positioning objective, you must consider:

- What position best fits your company culture, philosophy, and identity?
- What position best suits your product offering?
- Which position will best utilize your marketing efforts?
- What position gives you the greatest competitive advantage?

Choose a clear positioning objective, then write goals that will lead your company towards achieving this position.

Revenues

Dig out those annual statements and balance sheets from the last few years because you will need them here. This information will be crucial in the development of your sales revenue objectives. Obviously, you want to increase the sales revenue in some form, but by how much, and in what time frame? You can't know this without the data from your previous year's revenue.

Study and analyze the financial statements that you compiled and look for any patterns. What has been the percentage of increase/decrease in sales revenues? What has been your sales revenue average over the last 3-5 years? Have you experienced any seasonal fluctuations in sales revenues? This information about your past can be priceless in projecting the future.

There are multiple ways to interpret the data. You can also organize the information into different charts and graphs. Seeing the data represented visually sometimes gives you a different outlook. What you are looking for are identifiable trends within this data.

Decide what sales revenue goals are feasible for your company based on your analysis of the financial data. Don't limit yourself, be realistic about your potential. You can only expect so much growth within a given time frame, and usually, it won't deviate too much from the current patterns.

The best way to choose your goals for sales revenue is to assign a value (in increased revenue dollars) to each new variable that you expect to introduce. Your sales revenue is at a certain level now, because of your current internal activities, as external events that are beyond your control. In the future, you will attempt to "prime the pump" with new internal controls. How many additional sales do you expect from these controls? How can potential external variables possibly affect your sales and revenues?

Let 's say that you plan to launch a new product that you believe has the potential to sell 50,000 units within a three-year period. If this product retails for $5.00 per unit, then the value this adds to your projection is $250,000 (50,000 units * $5.00 each). On the other hand, you also expect that a rise in the production cost of your existing product will result in a $30,000 decline in sales revenue. Since the value of this variable is negative, it must be subtracted from your projection. This is a simple example, but it expresses the point that you can assign values to any stimuli (internal or external) that may affect your future sales revenues. To develop the most accurate sales revenue goals, consider all the variables that you feel could make a difference in your future earning potential. Then add or subtract their value from your current sales revenue average to form on point projections.

To be more precise, you can write separate goals for sales and revenues. Your sales goals will pertain to specifically to the number of units that you plan to sell in a period. Base your revenue goals on the amount of income that you expect from your sales activities. If you sell several products at different price points, specify how much you plan to sell of product A and how much of product B. If you offer upgrades or add-ons for additional costs, make goals for these as well. Adding specifications like this lets everyone in your organization know what exactly is expected of them so that accountability for every department is crystal clear.

You can use several different forms of measurement to write your goals. It can be a specific figure that you want to reach in a certain period or a percentage of increase over a certain period. You can set time parameters in months, quarters, or years. Go with whatever is easiest for your particular business situation.

Take an upside-down pyramid approach when choosing these goals. Start off with heavy detail for the first year, breaking down the goals by month or by quarter. That way you can micromanage your progress. Then, as you plan further out in time, get broader and switch to semi-annual, annual, or bi-annual time frames.

Example:

Objective -- Sustain continuous growth through enhanced sales.

Short Term Goals:

- Increase quarterly sales 4% by the end of the 2nd quarter, 20xx
- Increase quarterly sales 7% by end of 3rd quarter, 20xx
- Achieve monthly revenue of $12,000 by the end of April, 20xx
- Achieve monthly revenue of $16,000 by the end of July, 20xx

Long-Term Goals:

- Sell a total of 300,000 units of product A and 50,000 units of product B within 4 years.
- Earn $1,750,000 of total revenues within 5 years.

Profits

Now that you've set up the parameters of your sales and revenue goals you can establish what profits you expect to make from them. You may already have a profit margin that you are accustomed to, but it can always be improved. Your operation can become more efficient diminishing costs over time, manufacturing procedures can also be streamlined resulting in lower costs, raw materials could become less expensive, new and cheaper materials may become available, and if nothing else, prices can always be adjusted if the market will bear it. All of these variables will affect your profit margin.

There is no shortage of ways that profit margins can be manipulated. Knowing this, you should strive to increase your margins in any way possible. Your objective should always be to extract maximum profits out of each dollar of revenues. The goals here will be straightforward and simple.

Example:

Objective – Achieve a profit margin that is higher than industry average. Maintain this margin indefinitely.

Short Term Goals:

- Analyze current manufacturing procedures and find 4 ways that efficiency can be improved.
- Analyze current operating procedures and 4 ways that efficiency can be improved.
- Test the new procedural ideas for feasibility and potential cost savings.
- Test a higher price point to see if market will bear it.
- Choose the most viable solution for immediate implementation.

Long-Term Goals:

- Fully implement new manufacturing and operation procedures.
- Maintain lowest possible costs maximizing profits.

Product Mix

In its current state, your business might be limited in its offerings. In the future, you may want to expand on the products or services you offer now. Enhancing your product mix is a natural part of the progression and growth of your business; therefore, it is in your best interest to plan for these changes.

Developing additional products or services that compliment your current offerings can open doors to new markets and new sources of revenue for your company. For example, a dealer that starts off selling new computers decides to begin selling refurbished computers and offering repair services as well. By adding not only a new product but also a new service, this company has taken advantage of additional available market opportunities. You should consider doing the same with your offering.

Improve your product mix by adding a service that supplements your product, or vice versa. Also, you can offer new products or services in addition to your existing products or services to expand your mix. Bottom line, when thinking about the future of your company, you must plan to evolve your offerings to serve the market best.

Example:

Objective - Diversify product/service offerings to take advantage of all viable market opportunities. Maintain an optimal product mix.

Short Term Goals:

- Conduct research to locate new markets that we can strategically serve.
- Begin development of new Product A by October, 20xx
- Complete prototype of Product A by July, 20xx
- Complete testing of Product A by December, 20xx
- Bring Product A to market by April, 20xx

Long-Term Goals:

- Build a complete line of products that satisfies the needs of new-found markets.
- Develop and implement highly profitable supplementary services that will enhance our products.

- Create market research division to continuously search for new market opportunities.

Market Share

This category will probably take some research on your part. Here you need information on the size of the market(s) you compete in, it's worth (in dollar value), and your share of it. The size of your market refers to how many potential customers are within it, the total amount of money spent in this market is its value, and market share is the percentage of total industry sales that your company controls. In the next chapter, we will fully explore market share, but now we'll focus on the overview.

Increasing your market share is how you grow your business. Obtaining a larger share means that your company is selling more products and making more revenue. It is not uncommon for the largest players in an industry to collectively command a market share upwards of 80% or more. These are usually giant cumbersome corporations that invest a large number of resources to maintain this share.

Don't fret though because most of these companies started off small just like you. It took them time and effort to build a larger share. Further, in today's information-driven economy, technology has balanced the playing field more than ever. With vast lines of communication so wide open it is becoming easier and cheaper to reach potential customers. If you are strategic and creative in your execution, you could see rapid and exponential growth for your business. Even though you may not possess the cache of resources that your larger competitor does you can still effectively compete for market share.

It is important to keep in mind the size of your company when setting the goals for market share. The proportion needs to be correct. If you currently enjoy a 12% share of the market, your small business would probably be overwhelmed by an increase to 60% in 18 months. Your operation is just not big enough yet to handle this level of demand. You won't be equipped to serve this many customers.

Now, this doesn't mean that you should truncate your ambitions. You can still plan to control as much of the market as you wish. You have to take it in realistic steps. When your share increases, you must expand your operation to meet these new needs. As your company continues to grow in this way, you will be able to command even larger shares until you become the market share leader if that's what you desire.

Example:

<u>Objective</u> - Become a top 5 leader in market share

Short Term Goals:
- Improve market share by 7% after first fiscal year.
- Build market share to 15% after 24 months.

Long-Term Goals:
- Achieve market share of 28% overall within 5 years.

∞

This completes the first part of your marketing plan. By now, you should have a comprehensive profile of your enterprise. Its identity should be crystal clear. You may have even discovered some things about your business that you didn't know before. This is good! You're making progress.

This is a great start to your planning efforts. Writing the rest of the plan will be just as smooth. We'll continue this way, one part at a time, and before you know it, you will have a complete plan ready to be executed.

Next, you will profile the market itself by completing a market analysis. The point here is to improve your perspective and enhance your predictive abilities. When you are done with this part, you will be able to recognize potential and best decide which opportunities to pursue immediately.

Chapter 5:
Marketing Plan Part Two
Market Analysis

You can't become a leader in market share unless you first understand the competition in your chosen market. To get a complete analysis, you have to identify the unique characteristics of your market. This inside picture of your industry will reveal the needs, demands, and trends within it. Building an intimate knowledge of the market helps you to make highly effective strategic decisions and maneuvers.

Industry leaders always pay close attention to the market and follow the demand. They only produce those goods and services that are demanded by the people. Smart companies increase their market share by understanding the nature of customer needs and finding new ways to offer value. When your company makes it to the top, the only way to remain there is to evolve with the market, and continuously accommodate ever-changing demands.

Staying up-to-date with the state of your market is crucial, but it' s not always easy. In the information, age preferences change all the time because people are constantly being made aware of new options. Just when you think you have a good grasp of what's going on in the market, it shifts. Therefore, your company has to keep itself updated by continuously hitting the "refresh button" on your market analysis.

In business, the philosophy is: "adapt or die." Being a rigid and inflexible company only heightens your propensity for failure. Since you can't control the market, you have to let the market control you, and give the people what they want. Become a learning organization, embrace progression, and stay prepared for change.

This chapter's focus is on market analyzation. We begin by completing a SWOT analysis of your company. Then, you will learn how to conduct the research that produces high-quality information about your market. Next, we'll cover the enhancing qualities of market testing. Finally, you'll learn how to find potential competitive advantages based upon this information.

The market analysis provides details that are integral to your planning; In the previous chapter, while setting your market share objectives, you briefly explored a few of your industry's characteristics such as size and value. In this section, you will conduct research and collect additional information about your market, creating a panoramic view. Once you decipher the market's code, you will be able to best plan the strategies to penetrate the market and defeat the competition.

Situational Analysis

It's time to give your business a physical check-up. The analytical tool you will use is the situational analysis. Also known as a SWOT analysis, this classic marketing concept helps you to realize the Strengths, Weaknesses, Opportunities, and Threats of your business. It is a highly critical measure of potential.

S.W.O.T

Strengths, Weaknesses, Opportunities, Threats

The key to an accurate SWOT analysis is to be realistic and brutally honest with yourself. Remove the rose-colored glasses and take a long hard look at your enterprise from the inside out. Identify the internal strengths/weaknesses your company possesses and explore the external opportunities/threats you face from the environment. These four elements will give you a thorough situational analysis.

Situational analysis enhances your marketing strategy. It gives you an idea of all the positive and negative potential surrounding your business. Strengths are to be emphasized, cultivated, and utilized to your advantage. Weaknesses are to be realized at least but improved upon if possible. Opportunities are to be capitalized on, and threats must be prepared for and addressed. A SWOT analysis is an absolutely necessary part of your marketing plan.

When identifying the strengths and weaknesses of your business consider the following:

- Cost of Production
- Efficiency of Your Operation
- Marketing Skills
- Financial Resources
- Company/Brand Image
- Management Ability
- Company Assets (Physical and Intellectual)
- Information Cache
- Employee Skill/Know1edge
- Available Technology

Keep your assessment grounded in reality though. Be sure not to exaggerate your strengths and underestimate your weaknesses. You must be absolutely candid. Otherwise, your analysis won't be useful. If you fail to identify strengths correctly, you diminish your ability to take advantage of them. Disregarding weaknesses leaves your company vulnerable and unaware of where to direct improvement efforts.

When exploring possible opportunities and threats consider:

- Political Atmosphere

- Economic Fluctuation (domestic and Foreign)

- Weather Conditions

- Natural Disasters

- Unnatural Disasters (Man Made)

Opportunities exist in every environment; you just have to be able to recognize them. Optimists and creative thinkers are usually best at this, but you don't have to be born this way. With practice and experience, you can develop the ability to find viable opportunities in the most unlikely situations. If you think pragmatically, you will be able to see diamonds where your competitors see coal.

For example, in the past, lenders did not process sub-prime micro loans (small loans to consumers with bad credit). Traditional bankers thought the profit margin was too low for the work involved. One lender realized the opportunity and potential in this virtually untapped market, and payday loans were born.

Today there are payday loan locations on almost every corner (especially in poorer neighborhoods); doling out high-interest short-term loans to low-income customers. The interest rate is justified by the risk, and the high-profit margins that result are very lucrative. Removing morality from this example (because some regard this business model as predatory lending), these companies provide a legitimate service to people who are in demand of it. The first payday lending company found a niche and capitalized on an opportunity that others overlooked; now this industry is booming.

As a small business owner, you cannot afford to miss opportunities to create advantages and carve out your own niche in the market. This is how you not only compete but win against your larger counterparts--be more creative than them! The right opportunity can change the fortune of your company. Identify as many opportunities as possible, then decide which ones are viable.

Just as opportunities can be found everywhere, threats can come from anywhere. If you were psychic you would be somewhere winning the lottery every day not reading this manual; therefore, you must make your best guess as to what potential threats exist out there. Understanding the environment as it pertains to your business will help you to make educated guesses instead of wild assumptions. The better you become at foreseeing potential threats, better you can safeguard your company from being adversely affected by them.

You can focus about 70% of your threat assessment on the competition. This is because they are usually engaged in some activity with your demise in mind. Anything from the innocent development of a rivaling product, to underhanded corporate espionage, can be perceived as a threat from the competition. Later in the marketing plan, you will be able to fully assess the competition and develop a strategy specifically for this.

Even though the majority of your threats will come from the competition, Outside events can affect your business as well. Since these are less predictable, you must stay informed and be aware of the atmosphere. Read the newspaper, watch the news, and know what is going on in the world. If you are up-to-speed on current events, you can use your creative thinking skills to then decipher what the implications might be for your business.

Then, the housing market crashed, it was a major threat to most real estate investors. Property values plummeted in many areas, and people weren't buying houses like they used to. The investing companies that planned well and foreseen this threat were hurt the least. They gave themselves the best chance to survive this downturn by helping their customers find creative financing options, or transitioning over to renting the properties they couldn't sell. Those companies not so "quick on their toes" took a major hit and may not exist today.

Competent threat assessment is the prerequisite to effective crisis management. This can save your company from the brink of disaster. Since you can't see into the future, you can't possibly prepare for every potential threat. The best you can do is analyze the environment and make educated guesses as to what may be headed your way.

Situational analysis is an important first step in analyzing your market as a whole. It gives you an internal check of your company's attributes and an external view of the environment's potential. With this knowledge, you can strategize on how to utilize your strengths best, compensate for your weaknesses, capitalize on opportunities, and minimize threats.

Finding Your Competitive Advantage

The "strengths" and "opportunities" portion of the SWOT analysis should give you a great idea of potential competitive advantages. Those areas where your company is the strongest can be advantageous to you if your competitors are weaker in these areas. Opportunities that exist in the market can be exploited to create advantages as well. In today's hyper-competitive business atmosphere finding advantages is absolutely necessary if you want to stay in the game for the long run.

There are three main types of competitive advantages that exist:

- Cost

- Product/service differentiation

- Niche Strategy

Each of these elements has the power to give you a huge leg up on the competition, but each requires a unique philosophy, marketing strategy, and operating system. For this reason, you shouldn't try to exploit more than one type. Focus on the one most closely aligned with the strengths of your business.

Cost

If you can produce your product offering for a lower cost than your competitors, it is a definite advantage. Cost advantages usually stem from efficiency in the manufacturing process, efficiency in operations (labor and administrative costs), less expensive raw materials, product re-engineering, innovations, low overhead, or experience curves (becoming better producer with experience). To capitalize on this advantage, you can pass the cost savings on to the consumer by offering a lower selling price than your competitors, or you can maintain the market price and keep larger profits. If you are going to focus on cost efficiency be sure not to sacrifice quality, this can surely backfire!

Product/Service Differentiation

Your product offering can be better than the competition's, or it can be just different. Both offer advantages. If you can honestly say your product is functionally superior to your competitor's, then there is an obvious advantage--your product is the clear choice because it is superior. But there is still an advantage to being just different. Through branding, creative advertising, and promotions, you can persuade consumers to prefer the particular attributes your product offers over that of the competition. The key to using differentiation as an advantage is building preference.

Niche Strategy

Niching is the best option for small business with limited resources looking to gain an advantage over larger competitors. Targeting a small niche of the market creates an opportunity to control that segment. While the competitors are occupied trying to serve the larger market, you can be extremely focused on being the best at serving a particular segment. This option makes sense for companies that offer highly specialized or custom products to specific customers. The segment your serving has got to be large enough, with enough spending power to be viable though. For example, a company that specializes in producing authentic army boots for civil war reenactors probably won't have many competitors and can become superior at serving the needs of this niche.

Sustainable Competitive Advantages

The measure of any competitive advantage is its sustainability. Can it be maintained indefinitely, or is it just temporary leverage? When you are looking for advantages, your overall objective should be longevity. You want something that plays to your strengths and that you can continuously control.

Sustainable competitive advantages are unique and difficult to duplicate. This means that you must be creative in finding them. When your competitors are having problems matching it, and just can't do it the way you do, then you know that you have found a competitive advantage that is sustainable.

Part of sustaining a competitive advantage is not getting too comfortable with it. No matter how good an advantage may be, you must realize that it is always at risk. Your competitors will be working non-stop to close the gap you've created, so you can't get content, you must stay vigilant. If you have a cost advantage, keep looking for innovative ways to lower costs across the board. If you are a product differentiator, keep finding ways to make your product offering stand out from the competition. If you serve a particular niche, continue improving your stronghold on that segment.

In your marketing plan, elaborate on what you've found your competitive advantage to be. List different ways you can exploit it to increase its effects. Finally, explain how you plan to maintain this advantage over the long term.

Market Research

Take a moment to visualize your home. Now, using only your memory, try to draw a diagram of it. List the rooms, label the doorways, locate the appliances as specific as you can. Now, go ahead and compare it to the actual floor plan of your home. How close were you? Odds are, your rendition was a reasonably accurate representation.

Ok, that was easy, but what if you were asked to draw a blueprint of your home from memory? Would you be able to do that? Not so easy right? Even though you live there every day, you most likely don't know the exact dimensions of each room, the schematics of the wiring, the specifics of the plumbing system, or the location of the load bearing beams. To get these types of specifications, you would have to get your hands dirty and begin taking some measurements--you would have to conduct some research.

The same rule applies for your market. If you want the detailed information required to create a blueprint of the market, you must do some research.

From a bird's eye macro view, all the way down to ground level micro view, there is a vast amount of knowledge to be obtained about your market. You can give yourself the best perspective by collecting as much information as possible. You will be looking for data about market status, size, value, trends, product lifecycle, and competition. The knowledge you gain from your market research will give you an idea of what actions are necessary to penetrate the market.

Market Status

Markets have personalities of their own. Depending on its sensitivity to the environment and other stimuli, a market's status can vary widely. One of your first research tasks is to determine the current status of your market.

A market can be in one of several status distinctions: emerging, stable, or contracting (declining). Markets tend to start slow, expand rapidly, plateau, then begin to decline. The best time to enter a market is in the expansion stage. This is when opportunities are most abundant.

You can determine the status of your market by looking at its history. How old is the market? If it has been in existence for a while, how has it evolved? What has been the behavior and tendencies of those within this market? How long will their needs be relevant? These are all great indicators of the current status of your market. If you don't know this market status information already, research it online or try to interview another industry professional.

Sometimes you will find that your market is completely dependent on another for survival. The waffle cone industry cannot exist without the ice cream market; take away computer hardware, and software sales would plummet down to zero; if we all stopped wearing collared shirts, the tie market would suffer greatly. When your chosen market is dependent on another, note this in your marketing plan as part of your market's status.

Market Size

This is the measure of how many potential customers exist in the market you serve. Part of figuring this out is knowing the area your market covers. A market can extend from a local level to a global level, and anywhere in between. Of course, the larger the area, the more potential customers that will be in it. To be more detailed, separate the entire market into levels. Within a global market, there is a national market, a regional market, a state market, an inner-state regional market, a city market, and maybe even a side-of-town market.

Each level will have a certain population of people or businesses (for b2b companies) within it. Of this population, the number of those with the desire and the means to purchase your product defines the size of the market at this level. For example, if your company sells tractors, then out of all the business in a particular area, your market will be made up of only farms.

Thanks to the census, obtaining population numbers is relatively easy. You can visit www.census.gov to find the population numbers of any area. The website also segments the data demographically (age, income, gender, etc.). Using a simple demographic basis, you can determine how many, out of the total population, are potential customers. Using this method, you will be able to develop your estimates that will be exceptionally accurate.

Market Value

You can derive the value of a market from the total amount spent by the customers in the market. You can usually find this information through an organization such as the Bureau of Labor Statistics (www.BLS.gov), or the National Trade Professional Association (www.associationexecs.com), or the American Marketing Association (www.marketingpower.com). They've already spent the time doing the primary research, and have compiled these figures for you. All you have to do is find them.

If you are having trouble locating these numbers because your industry is not covered, you may have to develop your own estimate. You will base this estimate on the market size you found in the previous heading. Take the market price (the price that is normally charged) for one unit of your product/service and multiply it by the estimated number of potential customers in the entire market. Since market value is calculated on a yearly basis, you will need to multiply by how many times per year customers purchase one unit of your product.

> (Market Price) x (Market Size) x (Number of Avg. Yearly Purchases) =
>
> ## Market Value

This is a simplified version of the actual calculations that can be made to determine market value. If you choose, you can write a formula that is much more precise and exact by taking other variables into account (economic implications, deducting the percentage of consumers who are not current customers, accounting for sales of adjacent or alternative products, etc.). The above formula will give you a number that is workable though and will be adequate for our purposes here.

Your Share of the Market

Now that you know how much your market is worth, you can determine your company's share of it. If you recall, market share is the percentage of total sales that your business controls. If your business is currently in operation, then you own some percentage of the market. You need to know this number so that when you build upon it, your progress can be quantified.

There are two measures of market share: unit and revenue. Calculate revenue market share by dividing your year-to-date sales revenues by the total value of the market. Convert the decimal to a percent, and this is your revenue share of the market.

To find your unit market share divide the number of units you've sold year-to-date by the total number of units sold in the market.

Again, convert the decimal to a percent to get your unit market share.

Your YTD Sales Revenues ÷ Total Value of the Market =

Your Market Share %

Trends

Market trends are notions that a market is headed in one direction or another. Things like preference changes, style updates, new ideas, innovations, new technologies, economic fluctuations, current events, or publicity can all have an effect on a market. These variables can create needs and demands-- they have the ability to start or end a trend.

Unfortunately, there is no specific way to measure a market for potential trends, but to a trained eye, they can stand out. The most common indicators of a market trend are rapid increases in market size, market value, units sold, and competition. If you pay close attention to the market and learn to read between the lines, you may be able to notice trends early. This head start cab gives you a great advantage over your competitors.

Being the first to recognize a trend offers the best opportunity to capitalize on it. You will have the first chance to either serve new found needs or get out of a market that is on the decline. Years ago, many cellular service customers indicated to the market that they were sick of being locked into long-term contracts. Consumers wanted cellular service without the constraints of 2-year agreements. Metro PCS was one of the first companies to notice this trend, and they saw it as an opportunity to serve the demands of a new niche. The no-contract cellular company capitalized off of this trend to perfection. For years, they were able to command a large share of the market niche that resulted from this trend.

By paying attention to the market, finding a trend, and just giving the people what they wanted, Metro PCS was able to achieve prosperity. Today they directly compete with the giants of the cellular industry. Your company can do the same if you can spot trends in their earliest stages. Any potential trends that you are aware of now put them in this section of the marketing plan so that they can be considered as part of your market penetration strategy.

Product Life-Cycle

It's important for you to know where your product is in the life cycle. Since markets are directly affected by-products, this is crucial information to a market analysis. Product life cycle has four stages: introduction, growth, maturity, and decline. Each stage in the life-cycle has different marketing implications.

Each stage in the product lifecycle has unique characteristics.

Stage One: Introduction

- High Marketing Costs
- Low public awareness
- Slow sales growth
- High production costs
- Requires long management commitment

Stage Two: Growth

- Market size increases
- Rapid increases in sales growth o More distribution

channels appear

- Focus shifts from creating general awareness of product category to building awareness of specific brands
- Competition flood into market

Stage Three: Maturity

- Market size stagnates
- Sales growth slows and starts to decrease
- Competitors begin dropping off, but ironically competition gets more fierce
- Price wars shrink margins
- New innovations and reengineering becomes prevalent
- More niche markets are found in an attempt to take advantage of increasingly limited opportunities

Stage Four: Decline

- Consumer tastes have changed
- Sales drop significantly
- The only way to survive is to eliminate all non-essential marketing expenses.

Note where your product is in the life-cycle currently. Also, elaborate on the specifics of the situation.

Competition

You will study your competition in depth later on in the marketing plan (see marketing plan part five in Chapter #9). As for now, you will just acknowledge that they exist. In this part, you are only looking to list your direct and indirect competitors by name as a part of your market analysis.

You directly compete with those who operate in the same market area as you. Not only are they in close proximity, but they also offer the same product that you do. No matter their size, direct competitors will be trying to steal customers from you and constantly battle you for market share. They pose the most threat, so they get the most attention.

Indirect competitors sell similar, but different product offerings. Even if they do sell the same product, they operate outside of your market space. You are not necessarily fighting direct competitors for the same customers or market share, but they still need to be acknowledged. Even though they are not a direct threat now, they could expand into your territory, or vice versa, and become a problem later. Collecting information on them now could prove valuable in the future.

Locate all of your competitors and categorize them as direct or indirect. List them briefly by name in this section. You can also give each a threat level score of 1 to 5 so that you know where to direct your attention.

Market Testing

The reason you conduct market research is to get a better understanding of your market's characteristics. Market testing is a great supplement to this information. These are tests of a market's viability and will help you decide whether you should enter a market or get out of it.

Entering a market is risky. Many things can go wrong, and you could end up wasting a plethora of resources pursuing unworthy opportunities. Testing a market first will significantly reduce the risk an ensure that your pursuit has promise.

For our purposes, market testing will extend beyond just the market itself. You will be able to perform tests of the public's receptiveness and level of demand for your potential offerings. Also, you will test your company's ability to serve this market.

Market Tests

Market testing is about finding out how much opportunity is in a market. It gives you an idea of your potential for success. You will test the market for ease of entry, potential profit margin, and longevity.

Entering most markets only requires a certain investment and a determination to succeed. Some markets though, have barriers to entry. Government regulations, heavy competition, high investment requirements, licensing requirements, or contract needs are examples of barriers to entry.

For instance, if you wanted to develop a computer operating system, you would find that there are some major barriers to entry for this market. First, there are a few huge companies who completely control this market. If you posed a credible threat, they would try to crush you with the size, resources, and influence. Second, all computer manufacturers are already locked into contracts with these companies to use their mainstream operating systems exclusively. You would have a difficult time getting any computer manufacturer to switch to your new an unknown operating system. These barriers make it extremely tough to enter this market.

What kind of profit margin can you expect from this market? This is another crucial test. Certain industries have naturally high or low-profit margin potential. Grocery has a notoriously low-profit margin, while jewelry is known for its high margins. When you are considering a particular market, you want to know the average profit margin that is being earned in it. This helps you decide if it's worth the work getting into a market.

The longevity test is a question of how long a market could be in existence. In this test, you have to consider the current status of the market (emerging, expanding, stable, declining) and how fundamental the need is that it serves. You can depend on the automobile and housing markets to be around indefinitely because these are essential needs. Tablet computers and cable television won't have the same longevity because they are non-essential products and are at risk to be replaced with new technology. Both long lasting and short-lived markets can be taken advantage of, but for strategic purposes, you need to know which you are dealing with.

Consumer Tests

When you are trying to develop or introduce a new product offering to a market, you need first to test the consumers who you hope will be purchasing it. Testing them is how you learn what they need, what they desire, and what they prefer. Consumers will give you all the information you require if you provide them with a platform to express themselves. Within their opinions and criticisms is golden datum that you can use to serve their needs better.

There are various ways to extract valuable information from consumers such as:

- **Questionnaires:** A prepared list of questions. Intended to survey the public. You can ask them about their lifestyle, benefits, preferences, demographics, and anything else relevant to your purposes. If you use more close-ended questions, you will get results that are easier to measure. Conduct these surveys in any public setting (malls, parks, special events, etc.), over the phone, online, or in a closed setting.

- **Samples:** A small amount or trial version of your product. It is given to consumers to test their like or dislike of it. When giving samples, also try to record how people use the product. Include a post-use questionnaire to get the most information possible.

- **Mailshots:** Sending samples, letters, or marketing literature, by mail (or e-mail), to potential customers in a certain area. In your solicitation letter, you ask the target to respond to show their interest.

- **Focus Groups:** Compiling a group of target customers together in one place with the intention of asking questions distributing samples, and observing reactions. Use a questionnaire to collect information from participants, but also, video record the session if possible. This way you can also capture important body language cues and any interactions between members of the group.

- **Exhibits or Trade Shows:** Special showcase events designed for exhibiting products to consumers. You will show them how it's made, how it works, explain the benefits of it, and test interest. This works very well with b2b (business—to—business) companies because trade shows are often frequented by other business owners.

- **Pilot Study:** Debuting a product a small area to test people 's receptiveness to it and willingness to buy. For obvious reasons, the area you choose as the pilot should contain a significant number of your target customers.

These are all excellent ways to test the consumers in your market. With any of these methods, you will be able to gather a large amount of intelligence about the people who may be interested in buying your product offering. Use this intel later in developing products that people demand and value.

Company Capabilities Test

The final test of a market isn't a market test at all--it's a test of your organization's ability to enter market effectively. Is your company capable of serving this market? If so, is it structured to succeed here? Answer these questions by taking a look at your company.

You need resources to operate in any market, but does your company have the right resources? Financial, equipment, inventory, affiliations, and logistics are all resources that can make the difference between success or failure in a market. To perform well in certain markets, you need to possess certain resources. Owning equipment is important for manufacturing companies, while supply chain strength is necessary for those who want to enter a retail market. See if your company's available resources match with the resources needed to thrive in your chosen market.

An organization is only as good as those who run it. The caliber of your staff, especially management staff, has implications for your company' s capabilities. If you have any specialists or experts on your team, think about the advantage they may provide. Is their expertise relevant to the market your entering? What kind of value do they add? How can you use their expertise? It would be a major benefit to a company entering the security industry to have a former police captain as a part of their administration. Consider the skills that your staff possesses before entering any market.

Before investing your time and attention in a market, you should test your organization to see if you have the capabilities to win there. Be sure you have adequate staff and resources for the market you compete in. If you find that you lack in either of these dimensions, you need to strengthen them or possibly switch to a market where you have advantages.

Analyzing Market Information

You know what information to look for and how to find it, but how do you interpret it? The same data can have vastly different meanings to different organizations. Your objectives will largely depend on your company's direction. Even though the way your organization interprets data will be unique, there are some universal implications of market data.

Your SWOT analysis provided some insight into your company as well as the external environment. Treat the strengths you found within the company as assets. Think about how you can use them to get ahead. Acknowledge any weaknesses that your company has so that they don't become an Achilles heel that can be potentially used against you. Take advantage of the opportunities you've identified by utilizing your strengths. If you have to choose between two opportunities, select the one with the most promise and least amount of opportunity cost. If you do not prepare for them, threats can be very dangerous to your organization. When you find one, understand it and how it may affect your company.

There are certain opportunities that exist at every stage of a market's status. Of course, there are more opportunities in the expanding stage than in the declining stage, but there is revenue to be had in both. Once you determine the status of your market, consider what it means for your company. Emerging markets are largely untapped and ripe for any company, with the resources, to come in and take the lead. Expanding markets are saturated with competitors but also saturated with customers who provide abundant sales revenue. Even though stable markets have stopped growing, there is still a substantial demand to be fulfilled. Lastly, declining markets are not choice, but there are opportunities for efficiently lean companies that can re-invent the existing product offerings and create new value for customers.

Market size is an indicator of a market's strength. More potential customers mean more money is flowing through the market. You should only focus on the size of the level that your company can feasibly serve. If you operate a single hair salon in a small town, the target customers that exist within a 50-mile radius would be your focus, not the national haircare market. With market size, the key is to be sure there are enough customers in it to sustain your business.

Market value tells you how much money is flowing through a market. As with market size, more is better, but you can also count on competition to increase with the value of a market. The main thing to consider here is the potential revenues to be had. How much of that value can you expect to command?

Your current share of the market, if you're already in business, is indicative of how well you've done so far. You don't need to own a majority share of the market to be considered successful. It depends on how many competitors are in the market and their size. As a small enterprise, owning a five percent share in a highly competitive market could be exceptional; especially in a big market with enormous value. Establish context by comparing your market share with those of your competitors of similar size.

All perceived market trends are not created equal. Not everyone that you come across is worth the attention it takes to capitalize on it. The trends with the most promise will be those that shape attitudes, feelings, preferences, and needs. Trends not founded on genuine desire and demand won't have the power to move the market truly, and are not worthy of your time. It is important to recognize the difference between a bonafide trend and a short-lived fad because you cannot afford to waste your limited resources.

Your product's position in the life-cycle gives you an idea of how to market it and whether or not you should consider a transition. Marketing techniques at each level of the product life-cycle are unique; therefore, for strategic purposes, you need to understand where your product lies within it. If your product is in an unfavorable stage, you may want to think about choosing a new product.

Competition is a necessary evil of doing business. Yes. Competition can be fierce, and competitors want to put you out of business. But, on the bright side, competition keeps you on your toes and fresh. Competition can bring the best out of your company. Most importantly, competition only exists in markets where there are opportunities to be had. So, when looking at the competition in your market, don't get demoralized if there are many. It is not necessarily a bad sign.

When you tested your market, the purpose was to see how much promise it has. The objective was to quantify its potential. If you found your market to have many barriers-to-entry, this is usually not optimal. You want the easiest entry possible. After testing longevity, you should have found that markets with longer life expectancies are preferred over those with limited lifespans. As far as profit margins, high margin markets are great, but lucrative opportunities exist in lower margin markets as well. Interpret the meaning of your market test results based on your company's business model and unique operation.

You will find the information from your consumer tests to be particularly useful. If you listen, customers will tell you exactly what they want. As you learn more about their preferences, your product offering will naturally improve. Consumer tests are designed to help you gauge the "temperature" of your market, but you can also use the data to perfect your product and better cater to customer desires.

The company capabilities test results are mostly straightforward. Your organization is either prepared to take advantage of a market, or it's not. The good thing is you can always improve your position with staff upgrades or acquisition of additional resources. If you determine that you are truly incapable of serving the market that you've chosen, then you probably need to move on to a different one.

You have probably revealed a wealth of knowledge or information about your market through research and testing. Process this data to gain knowledge from it. Use your newly acquired knowledge to build the strategies that will allow you to control your market.

∞

After completing market research, the particulars of your market should be crystal clear. If you were analyzing this market to see if you should enter it, then by now, your mind should be made up. If you are already doing business in a market and you were looking for a better understanding of it, then you should have developed that. Either way, you can now call yourself an expert on your market, and when you are this familiar with an industry, your chances for success increase dramatically.

Now that you have become familiar with your market, you are ready to begin your takeover. The next chapter is about setting up your marketing mix elements. This is the heart and soul of your marketing plan. Manipulating your marketing mix is how you take advantage of all the opportunities that you have uncovered in your market analysis. We are only going to focus on the product, price, and place aspects in the following chapter. Promotion will receive special attention in the communications plan chapter.

Chapter 6:
Marketing Plan Part Three
Marketing Mix

O k, put on your consumer hat for a moment. As a buyer of goods and services, what do you personally value? Chances are, like most consumers, you value product offerings for more than just their utility. You value various benefits of not only the product itself but maybe even some factors of your purchase experience (convenience, availability, timeliness, etc.) as well.

Consumer values are not monolithic; they are multidimensional. It is shallow to think that consumers only value price or product usage, it is much deeper than that. Your customers will have many different things that they value, on many different levels. So, offering them total value means that you must find the proper marketing mix.

In this section of your marketing plan, you will work out the particulars of your marketing mix. You will decide what variation delivers the most value to your customers while keeping your operation efficient and profitable. The first three p' s (product, place, and price) of the marketing mix is our focus here. Once these elements are in place, you can decide how you should promote the product offering that you've created.

Product Strategy

The product offering is a fundamental aspect of your business. It is the center of all the marketing mix elements. Base any decision that your marketing department makes on the good or service that you offer. It is only appropriate that this element is considered first since the others depend upon it.

If your business is currently operating, then you have already developed a product offering. You should still review this section though, because you may find some ways to improve or upgrade your product. If you are planning your business from scratch, and haven't created your product offering yet, then this section will help you to get that done.

The functions that take your product from concept to completion are the begging of your product strategy. This includes product development and packaging. Just as important, are the intangibles of the strategy, like branding and positioning. If you plan a strong product strategy here, the result will be a quality product offering.

Product Development

The first step in building a product offering is creating a product. This is where your idea materializes into existence. For goods products, this means manufacturing of an actual unit. For service products, you will find ways to assist consumers with things they can't do, or don't want to do themselves. In both instances, the objective is to bring value to consumers.

The process of developing a product can become highly involved, requiring many activities and various decisions. Let's keep it simple though. For the purposes of this marketing plan, we will assume that you have already done the necessary research and decided what in-demand product(s) that you want to produce or provide. Further, we will assume that you have completed a full business analysis (checking the product to see if it makes business sense) and have created a working prototype for every one of your chosen goods or services.

Now, review each of your prototypes one at a time. Do they have the attributes that your target customers desire? Will the product(s) function adequately? Are they user-friendly? Critique your product concept(s) from end-to-end with the consumer in mind. The needs, wants, and preferences of your target customers should be the primary influence and inspiration of your product's design.

We must note that developing a product does necessarily mean inventing an entirely new product. Nor does it mean that you must manufacture a product on your own. This may not be a part of your business model. If you are a retailer, your product is convenience because you make available the products of many manufacturers in one place. If you are a book publisher, then your product is information. The product of lawyers, doctors, accountants, consultants, and other professionals is advice and expertise. No matter what you sell, it's all some kind of product, and you will use the same process in developing it.

In your marketing plan, write down all of the qualities your product has currently. If you came across some shortcomings in your product l s design, and will be implementing sane changes, note them here as well. Record all the specifications of your product offering. The purpose here is to ensure that your product(s) are well developed and prepared to realize their full potential.

Product Mix

Very rarely does an organization offer only one product. Most companies find it beneficial to sell a variety of offerings called a product mix. The term product mix refers to all the products that an organization has available for sale. The makeup of your product mix is one of the keys to your product strategy.

There are many different types of products that can be offered within a product category. This goes for goods as well as services.

The combination of offerings that your company decides to provide is what makes up your product mix.

> **For example:** A retail operation selling electronic goods can have a product mix that includes: computers, televisions, cellular phones, digital cameras, and other electronic equipment. This same retailer may also sell repair, delivery, and warranty services as another part of their product mix (sometimes called the service mix).

Product mixes can be broken down into individual product lines that contain specific product items that are closely related to one another. Each item within a product line serves the same consumer need but varies superficially. The level of diversity between the items is totally up to you. Creating different versions of the same product can potentially expand your target market, provide additional purchases. The athletic equipment company Nike has numerous product lines will include t-shirts that have a similar theme or style; but different sayings, artwork, colors, or sizes.

In the product development stage, you brought one or more types of product items into existence. Here, you will organize them into the product lines that will make up your product mix. If it is feasible, you will also be looking for ways to improve the depth of your product lines (by varying your product item(s)) and expand the width of your product mix (by adding new product types).

Packaging

Packaging, especially for goods, can be very important to your product strategy. This is a great example of how strategic decision exists in all aspects of business. When you think of packaging, usually you don't realize how much it is actually used for. Packaging serves several purposes including containment, protecting, promoting, and facilitating.

Packaging's main function is keeping products contained. Once a product has been manufactured, it must be placed in some type of package to signify that it is an independent unit. Products that have several pieces to a unit need to be packaged to keep the pieces together. This makes the units easier to ship and sell. For food products, packaging keeps perishables fresh, lists ingredients, and allows for consistent weight or count measurements.

Packaging is sometimes used to protect products as well. Shipping and handling can be treacherous, and most products are vulnerable to some type of damage or contamination. Packing can be designed to protect against these types of threats. Air is pumped into potato chips to keep them intact during shipping. Safety seals are placed on many medications to prevent tampering. The integrity of your product must be maintained at all costs, so protective packaging is crucial.

There are some facilitating qualities of packaging as well. Packaging can be designed for easier storage, easier shipping, easier opening, reclosing capability, easier use, recycling ability, biodegradability, and other accommodations. The goal is to facilitate simplicity from every aspect, particularly that of the final consumer. Can you remember what life was like before the easy squeeze ketchup bottle?

One of the lesser considered purposes of packaging is promotion. There are brand names, logos, slogans, trademarks, marketing messages, and many other types of promotional markings that can be placed on a package. Even color schemes are used strategically to be eye-catching and relay indirect messages to consumers (green colors can be interpreted as eco-friendly or organic). This is a great way to create differentiation. When a product is directly competing with other products on retailer shelves, promotional packaging is particularly important. The packaging alone could make the difference between a product being chosen or not.

It' s been well-established that packaging is much more than just product containment; therefore, it should be a deeply considered part of your product strategy. Packaging design is almost as important as your product design. Before you decide what to wrap your product in, plan all of the ways that you can use this packaging to maximize its effectiveness.

Branding

Now that you have developed a quality product that the market will desire, you need to build a strong brand behind it. Quality product/strong brand is a formidable combination and a definite formula for success in unit sales. Since we know that brands build preference, we can conclude that branding is a necessary supplement to a product strategy.

Building a brand requires a strategy of its own. It begins with the establishment of identity. Any distinctive characteristic of your product offering can be a part of its brand identity. This includes things like the design of the product itself, logos, slogans, taglines, packaging, color schemes, tastes, smells, processes and many other attributes.

Once you have given your brand an identity, it needs to be exposed to the public to create awareness. In all of your communication initiatives, you should be promoting the brand (covered further in Chapter 8: Marketing Plan Part Five). If you can get people to try the brand, you have a good chance of getting them to prefer the brand. Building preference for your brand is the overall goal of branding.

You should be constantly maintaining your brands. Their delicate image and integrity can be easily damaged by a single incident or some bad press. For this reason, you need to protect your brand by closely managing it. You cannot allow it to be associated with anything or anyone that's not in-line with its stated values.

Outline your branding strategy in your marketing plan. Explain your brand's identity, what it stands for, how you will promote it, and your plan to manage it. This way you will stay consistent with all your branding efforts and can remain focused on the objective.

Quality Assurances

Quality assurances, like warranties and guarantees, are essential components of your product offering. They build trust in the minds of consumers and take away the perceived risk involved with purchasing your product. When your product's quality is exceptional, or at least up to par, quality assurances can be a simple way to strengthen the public's perception of it. Offering a warranty and/or guarantee on your product shows that you have confidence in its craftsmanship and its ability to effectively serve the needs of the consumer.

Positioning

How you plan to position your product is a crucial decision. It will be the basis for your promotional platform. If you remember, a position is the image your product holds in the minds of consumers, and positioning is the process of shaping the public's perception of your product. There is no shortage of positions for you to use either (for more information, see Chapter 2: Marketing 101). Whatever position you decide is the most favorable for your product, establish it with marketing communications, then cultivate it by staying consistent with your actions and messaging.

In this section, give a full explanation of the desired position for each one of your products. Don't worry about how you are going to establish the position at this point, just focus on choosing the best position for your marketing objectives. Also, consider the image of your brand(s) before selecting a position so you can be sure that they coordinate with each other. Positioning is the final piece needed to sure up your product strategy. You should now have a total product offering that you can be proud of.

Place (Distribution) Strategy

With your product offering locked down, you can now focus on how you will deliver it to the market. Getting your product from the manufacturer to the consumer is about more than just logistics. Distribution is about convenience. You want to make it as effortless as possible to acquire your good or use your services. The easier it is for customers to get your product, the more units they will buy--it's that simple!

A good place strategy breaks down barriers that may get between your product and your customer. It makes your offering available on the widest scale possible. If consumers hate traveling so far to get your product, then make it available in their immediate area. If they don't want to leave home to buy your product, then sell it virtually (by phone, mail, or internet) and deliver it to their house. In your place strategy, you will be looking for ways to enhance the availability of your products by evaluating your service area, supply chain, and logistics plan. Your objective is to create a system of distribution that not only maximizes consumer convenience but also remains realistic for your company's operation.

As you are developing your place strategy, you should always keep your costs and available resources in mind. Of course, you would like your product offering to be available worldwide with stores in every city on the planet. It would be great if you owned a huge fleet of trucks and planes that shipped products from your various warehouses to each one of your retail locations around the globe. Unfortunately though, this is not feasible for the small business because of the resources required and the costs involved. You have to be realistic about what your company can achieve with the resources at your disposal. Further, to keep the price of your products in check, you need to keep costs down.

But...You cannot allow your limited resources to limit your distribution strategy. You can go as far as your creativity can take you. With an internet storefront, you can make your products available on a global scale. Through UPS, FEDEX, or DHL you can deliver your products anywhere. Your distribution system can be far-reaching and efficient, without being complex or costly.

The information age has created a global village where the entire planet is a huge network. This levels the playing field for your small business. With some creative planning, you can sell your products everywhere just like your competitors. The key is developing a place (distribution) strategy that takes advantage of these opportunities and extends your reach.

Service Area

How far will you reach? What are the areas that you want to service? This is pertinent information for your place strategy. By specifying your service area, you can know where to focus your service area you can know where to focus your resources. Essentially, your service area makes up your market.

Brick-and-mortar storefronts have a certain service area based on their physical location. Depending on the type of business you operate, you can't really expect customers to travel much more than 50 miles (in any direction) to visit your business. The rarer and unique your product offering is the further away people will come from.

Walt Disney World gets customers from around the world that come to patronize their business. This is because their product is the only one of its kind anywhere. In contrast, a retail store selling Disney merchandise will receive mostly local customers because it is not unique and more common. For your brick-and-mortar storefront, plan the service area to be within a certain radius of its physical location.

Virtual storefronts are a different story. Accepting orders over the internet or by phone extends your service area to anywhere that you can deliver your product offering. Although there is promise in servicing an area this large, you want to be sure that you can handle the additional administrative work it requires. You will need to seamlessly coordinate order taking, order filling, and order shipping on a consistent basis. The process has got to work the same way every time. Also, to be effective, you must research and completely understand each of the markets you are operating in.

Describe the service area for each of your storefronts. Make sure not to overreach. Stay within your capabilities. As your business expands, so will your reach, but in this section, focus on the present. This diagram of your service area will determine how you will execute the other elements of your place strategy.

Supply Chain Management

A supply chain is made up of all the intermediaries who are responsible for bringing a product from the producer to the end user. This can include any combination of manufacturers, agents/brokers, wholesalers, and retailers. When the collective members of a supply chain do their job and make products readily available to consumers, a supply channel is born. One of the objectives of your place strategy is to plan your role in an existing supply chain or build an entirely new supply chain with the hope of creating an efficient and consistent supply channel.

Your supply chain can be direct; where your products are sold straight from manufacturer to consumer or involved; where any number of "middlemen" can exist to move your product from manufacturer to consumer. No matter where your company lies in the supply chain, you want the least amount of links between you and the producer of the product as possible without sacrificing efficiency. Every hand that touches the product in transit to the end consumer increases costs and decreases your margin. This is why supply chain management is so important.

Evaluate your supply chain as it is currently constructed. How many intermediaries are between your business and the manufacturer? Identify any that may be unnecessary and devise ways that you can eliminate them. If you can build your own relationship with your supplier's supplier, you may be able to negotiate a better price than what you are currently paying. Be sure that you're capable of handling the additional responsibilities that come with moving up the chain though. Bypassing your normal supplier may mean that you have to purchase higher quantities of products to get that lower price, this increases your risk. If you're confident that you can still distribute this larger quantity of inventory effectively, then go for it.

The channel that you are going to use should match the product you are selling and the type of company you have. More complex, expensive, and customized products will require a direct channel, where you will sell directly to customers using a sales force (explained later in Chapter 11: Sales Plan). The products that are more standard and common can be sold using longer distribution channels with more supply chain intermediaries. Larger, resource-rich, companies are better equipped to utilize direct channels. Smaller companies benefit from the warehousing and sales assistance that intermediaries offer in an involved channel.

If you produce your own product, you will need to create an entirely new supply chain and distribution channel. Specify which channel type you plan to use based on which makes the most sense for your product setup. Also, detail how you plan to execute and why you will succeed using this channel.

Your challenge is to make the supply chain lean as possible without negatively affecting the channel. If you alter the chain in a way that benefits your company but damages the channel, everyone suffers. You don't want to do anything that will make the product less available, or less convenient. If you lose efficiency in the supply channel, you risk losing consumers as well. You can't afford to take this risk. You need to manage the supply chain first, for the benefit of the consumer, then for your own benefit.

Logistics

The logistics portion of your place strategy covers the physical distribution of products to consumers. You've got the supply chain set up, but how will the products actually move through it? How do you plan to receive products from your suppliers? Then, how will you deliver the products to your customers? You need to develop a system that will keep you supplied with just enough inventory to satisfy the demands of your customers.

The object of your logistical plan is to get products to your customers on time and in location. This is the true definition of convenience. Today's consumer expects their desired products to be available on demand. This indicates that the value of convenience is at an all-time high. The companies that can best accommodate consumers by offering the highest level of convenience, usually enjoy the most success.

Being timely basically means controlling outgoing and incoming inventory. When consumers decide that they are ready to satisfy their needs, at that moment, you must have what they want when they want it. Otherwise, they will go somewhere else to get it. Consumers will not wait for you to restock, and they may not trust you again to satisfy their demands. On the other hand, you know from your Accounting 101 class that you don't want to be sitting on an excess of inventory either. This ties up cash, and you don't want to be stuck with a surplus of depreciating units that you can't sell. Your aim is to maintain a level of supply that matches the level of demand and nothing more.

You can't get products to your centrally located storefront without transportation, the main function of logistics. After you purchase inventory from your supplier, you will need to schedule physical transport that will move it from their location to your location. This can be via truck, air, sea, or rail. Each has specific advantages and disadvantages. Water is low cost, but slow and not very accessible. Trucking is very reliable; accessible, and relatively fast, but can be costly. Air is exceptionally fast and easily traced but is very costly. Rail is moderately priced; accessible; highly capable, but very slow.

Weigh your options and come up with a method of transportation that will best suit your unique needs. It must consistently get your product inventory to you just in time and on location while being cost-efficient. Your strategy doesn't have to be a single method either; you may find it necessary or advantageous to use a combination of transportation types. Also, if you are going to offer delivery service, plan logistics for this as well. Figure out how you will transport your products to your customers.

Price Strategy

Price is one of the most valuable weapons in your marketing arsenal. Pricing can set you apart from the competition, offer you an advantage over the competition, or help you to establish a certain position. Price directly affects sales, revenues, and profit margins. The price element of the marketing mix has the power to make or break your product. Pricing has huge implications, and with so much riding on these decisions, you need to methodically develop a pricing strategy that will contribute to the success of your products.

While it is true that the price you choose has to cover your costs, this is not the only variable to consider in your pricing strategy. There is a delicate balance between the price that's right for the market and the price that's best for your bottom line. To find this elusive price you will need to ponder not only costs, but also value, profit margin, and competition. Use these variables together to create perfect prices for products that are mutually beneficial for and your customers.

Costs

A wise man once said: "It takes money to make money". Never a truer statement. Bringing your products to market has various attached costs. Some costs will be variable, and others will be fixed. Correctly assessing these costs is the most important task of your pricing strategy. It will be the basis for your final sales price.

The costs that vary based on the number of units produced are called variable costs. As your sales increase, so do your variable costs. Things like materials, labor, utilities (gas/electric), advertising, fuel, and maintenance, are all examples of variable costs. They are tied directly to sales volume and will fluctuate with production.

You will need to calculate your variable costs on a per unit basis on your way to developing a final price. To do this, first, find your total variable cost by the number of units. Then divide the total variable cost by the number of units produced at that cost. The resulting number is your per unit variable cost. The per unit variable cost will be used later in your pricing decision.

Total Variable Costs ÷ Number of Units Produced =
Variable Cost Per Unit

Regardless of how many units you produce and sell, fixed costs will remain the same. These costs are related to the everyday operation of your company. Doesn't matter the amount of business you conduct, costs like building leases; equipment leases; insurance; taxes; vehicle notes; telephone; or internet service will not change. That's what makes these costs fixed.

Total Variable Costs

Example - To produce and sell 1000 units of Product A variable costs (VC)	
Materials	$1,800.00
Freight	$500.00
Labor	$1,500.00
Energy	$150.00
Supplies	$100.00
Promotional Marketing	$400.00
Total Variable Costs:	**$4,450.00**

Total VC ($4,450) ÷ 1000 units produced = $4.45 Per Unit Cost

Fixed costs are usually paid out on a monthly basis. The best way to allocate them per unit is to divide the total number of units you produce in a week into your total weekly fixed costs. The resulting figure will be your per unit fixed costs.

Total Weekly Fixed Costs ÷ Number of Units Produced = **Fixed Cost Per Unit**

Total Fixed Costs

Example - To produce and sell 1000 units of Product A variable costs (VC)	
Building Lease	$500.00
Equipment Lease	$175.00
Company Vehicle Note	$50.00
Insurance (For Combined Assets)	$125.00
Salaries	$1,250.00
Total Fixed Costs:	$2,100.00

Total FC ($2,100) ÷ 1000 units produced = $2.10 Per Unit Cost

Your total cost per unit (TCPU) is made up of your fixed cost per unit (FCPU), plus your variable cost per unit (VCPU). This is an accurate measure of all the costs associated with producing one unit of your product. To break even, and avoid a loss, you will need to charge at least the TCPU as the sales price of your products.

FCPU (Fixed Cost Per Unit) + VCPU (Variable Cost Per Unit) =

Total Cost Per Unit

Example Total Cost Per Unit

Variable Cost Per Unit:	$4.45
Fixed Cost Per Unit:	$2.10
Total Cost Per Unit:	$6.55

Profit/Markup

Since you are not in business to break even, your sales price needs to include a margin over-and-above your total cost per unit. The strategy lies in finding the appropriate margin. This depends on your pricing objective. Will your focus be on profits or sales? If you are profit-oriented, then you will look for a higher margin. If you are sales oriented, you will set the margin lower with the hopes of selling more units.

The preferred method of markup is calculating the margin as a percentage of total cost per unit. This percentage can be in the hundreds, down to single digits. The industry average markup serves as the middle ground between a sales focused margin, and a profit-focused margin. If the average margin in your industry is 26%, then a sales-oriented margin would be somewhere between 12-20%. A profit-oriented margin would be between 31-50%.

Example – TCPU = $6.55 / Industry Average Markup 26%
Price A: Sales Oriented Strategy -- 18% Margin (Low)

- Selling Price $7.73 ($6.55 x 1 .18)
- Markup Amount $1 .08
- To reach revenue goal of $10,000 need to sell 1294 units
- Time required to reach goal 5 weeks @ 250 units per week (Low price sells more)

Price B: Profit Oriented Strategy -- 36% Margin (High)

- Selling Price $8.91 ($6.55 x 1.36)
- Markup Amount $2.36
- To reach revenue goal of $10,000 need to sell 1123 units
- Time required to real goal 17.5 weeks @ 150 units per week (High price sells less)

Cost based pricing needs first to cover your costs; then you will choose the most appropriate margin according to your objectives. The lower your markup, the more units you will sell (in theory), but the less you will make on each one. The higher your markup, the fewer units you will sell, but your profits will be higher for each unit. You have to decide which strategy will offer you the best advantage.

Market Value

Every product has a certain value attached to it. Part of the value is derived from the costs of the materials used to create the product, but part is personal. Each consumer values products differently based on things like use of the product, sentiment attached to the product, the image associated with owning the product, convenience the product brings to their lives, safety and security the product offers, and other factors. Even though consumer values differ, this is the market price.

Market price (or market value) represents the collective value that consumers have for a product, it's what the people in a market feel a product is worth. The market price for your product type must be considered as part of your pricing strategy. Compare your cost based price to the market value for your product to ensure that you are being realistic in your pricing. You might find that you need to adjust your price because it deviates too far away from market value.

Pricing your product above market value (referred to as skimming) is less common but can be effective. If you choose this pricing strategy, you need to have a reason why people should pay a price more than market value for your product. Better materials, superior craftsmanship, exceptional quality, standout service, uniqueness, or advanced technology are all attributes that could justify a higher price. Also, products that bring a certain level of prestige to an owner usually command a premium price as well. These products are considered high-end, and they target the consumers at the top of the market. Higher prices usually mean higher profits.

It is much more common for products to be priced around market value. This is because, in most markets, the bulk of the consumers reside in the middle of the market, which is reflective of the economic status of today's average consumer. Pricing your products at this level is a safe and simple strategy.

Selling your products at a price lower than market value is called penetration pricing. The objective of this strategy is to penetrate the market by moving a higher quantity of units. The target here is the bottom of the market, where a significant number of consumers are, especially in a troubled economy. There is a particular market position associated with selling below market value though. The further your products are priced under the market price; the more your company will be perceived as a "discount" type. This will attract a certain type of customer, but repel others.

Your examination of market value should reveal your cost efficiency. If your costs are well below market value, then you're very cost efficient, and your pricing options are wide open. You can utilize any pricing strategy that you like. As your costs get closer to market value, your options become more limited because you are less cost-efficient. If you find that your costs are too close, or exceeding market value, you can use a price skimming strategy as a temporary fix, but you will have to adjust your costs to improve efficiency.

Your costs should never be more than market value. This means that you are grossly cost inefficient, and you are spending too much producing your product. You will need to find ways to cut costs in your operation, to make your product production cheaper. These cuts will most likely come from variable costs like materials, labor, or selling expenses because they are the only ones that can be adjusted. If you can't get your costs under market value, then you may need to change your product offering choice.

Find the market value of your product type and use it to help you determine your price strategy. It serves as a measure of what price is too much, and what price is not enough. Record your products current market value in your marketing plan, and stay up-to-date with it.

Competitive Pricing

You know what costs you need to cover to make one unit of your product. You know what the market is willing to pay for your product. Now you need to know how your competitors are pricing their products. What strategy are they using? How will you counter? A large amount of competing is done on this level, so as you are searching for the right price you must consider it from a competitive standpoint also.

In our market war, competitive pricing is like hand-to-hand combat. You will trade pricing punches back-and-forth trying to knock each other out. The difference in price could be as small as mere pennies, but in highly competitive markets or commodity markets, even pennies can sway a customer' s purchasing decision. For instance, you need to purchase gas, and two stations are across the street from each other. One is selling gas for $3.47 per gallon, and the other is selling gas for $3.43 per gallon. Which would you choose?

Most likely you will go to the less expensive station. Since gas is a commodity, the only variable you consider is price, and when price is the only difference, cheaper always wins.

Compare your expected price with that of your closest competitors. How is it different? If it's much higher make sure you have a good reason why. If it is much lower, consider increasing it unless you are specifically using a low price strategy. You don't want to leave revenues and potential profits on the table if you don't have to.

Competitive pricing is about who can offer the most for the least price. If you are going to engage your competitors this way, look to keep your price at, or just below, their average prices and focus on continuously improving the efficiency of your operation. Whoever can best control costs will win the competitive pricing fight.

Other Factors

After considering costs, market value, and competitiveness, you will arrive at your best base price. This sales price will be well developed and should satisfy your objectives as well as your customers' expectations. It's not supposed to be set in stone though. You must be prepared to deviate away from your base price when the situation calls for it. Sometimes your strategy needs to include discounts, sales, and differential pricing.

There are various ways for you to offer discounts on your products. Cash discounts are given to customers for paying upfront (without financing) or paying on time. Bulk discounts are for customers who purchase products in larger than normal quantities. New customer and customer loyalty discounts can be used as incentives. Rebates are given for purchasing products during a certain time but must be redeemed by customers later after paying full price. Coupons give discounts off base price and are redeemed at the time of purchase. Good discount strategy encourages action and/or sells more units in a shorter time frame without altering your customer's pricing expectations.

Another form of discount is the sale. You may find it beneficial to host an occasional sale as a promotional tactic, and a way to liquidate inventory. You can start a sale with any attached theme. You can have a sale for a certain day of the week, a grand opening sale, an inventory sell-off sale, a charity sale, an anniversary sale, a holiday sale, or any number of other platforms. When you host a sale, you will inevitably cut into your margin, but the payoff will be increases in exposure and sales volume.

Your price can also differ based on geography. The price you charge for your product in New York City may not be the same as what customers in Detroit are paying. The economics of supply and demand in these two unique markets are dissimilar so you must adjust your prices to compensate. If you operate a business where your prices are negotiable, your prices will be adjusted as well. This is another example of differential pricing.

Base price sets the foundation for your pricing scheme, but there are opportunities in adjusting your prices in certain situations. Strategically altering your prices can offer you various advantages in the right circumstances. For this reason, you should stay flexible and change your prices as needed.

∞

The product, price, and place marketing mix elements will coordinate to create your total product offering. They will get the unique product that you've created on the shelves and ready for sale to the public. If you carefully plan your moves in each one of these initiatives your offerings will have great potential to bring success to your company.

The fourth marketing mix element, promotion, will introduce your strong product offering to the world. But before you can do this, you need to identify who you expect to purchase these products. This is your target market. In Chapter Seven, you are going to define your target market so that you know who you are going to be communicating with in your promotional strategy.

Chapter 7:
Marketing Plan Part Four:
Define Target Market

Every consumer is an individual. They each have unique personalities, values, behaviors, and preferences. You can sell your products to anyone, but you can't solicit to everyone; therefore, you need to establish one or more types of customers that you will focus on selling to.

As you were first developing your product, you had an ideal customer in mind. You had an idea of who would be most interested in, and most likely to purchase your products. Who are these people? In this section of your marketing plan you will identify and characterize your target customers.

The term target customers refer to the group of customers, with similar characteristics, that you plan to direct your marketing efforts on. Although each consumer is an individual, they can be grouped together using geographic, demographic, or psychographic commodities. These groups represent segment of a larger market. The purpose of grouping potential buyers this way is to attempt to communicate with them simultaneously on a level they can all relate to. Whichever segments you find offers the most opportunity to your organization will be your targets.

Your chosen targets have to be completely profiled so you can know how to best reach them. Understanding their unique characteristics will maximize your ability to communicate with them effectively. Because your small business has limited resources to devote to marketing communications, targeting will be inexplicably crucial to the success of your promotional strategy. When you are dealing with a smaller advertising budget, you will get less shots to reach consumers; thus, you must make each one count by precisely aiming and hitting your targets with supreme accuracy.

To best define your target market there is a process for you to follow; First; the overall market must be divided into workable segments that are in accordance with your company's marketing objectives. Next, you will select the segments that have the most promise, best opportunity, and where your advantage is the greatest; these are your target markets. Once you've identified your targets, you need to learn more about them by characterizing and completely profiling them. Finally, with this intimate knowledge of who your target is on a personal level, you can choose the communication methods that will not only reach them, but also move them to action.

Divide up the Market

Unless you sell a highly specialized product, your overall market is probably huge. Most likely there are a large number of potential buyers for your offering. You can try to reach all of them with a single mass communication campaign, but this is high cost and has a low conversion rate. This is why to be most effective you will need to divide up the market into sections that you can tailor your marketing messages to. It is extremely difficult to explore an entire ocean of consumers in the canoe that is your small business; however, if you separate this ocean into smaller more navigable segments, your exploratory ability increases.

Choose Segmentation Bases

Your market segmentation scheme will begin when you choose the bases upon which you will specify the segments. The three main bases that are used to divide markets are: geographic, demographics, and psychographics. Each of these bases are defined fully in Chapter 2 "Marketing 101 To recap though, geographic segmentation divides the market based on region, size, density, or climate. Demographic segmentation uses characteristics like age, gender or ethnicity to break up the market. Psychographic variables focus on the reasons why people buy. Usage rate, a less commonly used base, splits up the market based upon how much people buy.

Attached to each base is a set of defining variables:

- **Geographic -**
  - o Market Size: The area (in square mileage) that makes up a market.
  - o Market Density: The number of people within a given market area.
  - o Climate: The normal weather conditions of a market area (tropical, cold, rainy, dry, etc.).
  - o Region: An area that already exists on a map where the people have a particular culture, norms, attitudes, and way of life (Midwest, Eastern Seaboard, Northeast, etc.).

- **Demographic -**
  - o Gender: Sex of those within a market.
  - o Age: The age, in years, of those within a market.
  - o Income: Amount of annual income of the individual, or the household of consumers in a market.
  - o Ethnicity: The race, or ethnic backgrounds of the

people in a market (Caucasian, African American, Asian, Arabic, Hispanic, Etc.).

o Education: Level of education that the consumers have in market (high school diploma, some college, associate degree, etc.).

o Family Life Cycle: Covers marital status, number of children, and any other information about the home life of the consumers within a market.

- **Psychographic -**

o Personality: The types of personalities of the individualism a market (outgoing, humorous, extroverted, reserved, upbeat, serious, Etc.).

o Motives: The reasons people in a market have for buying products.

o Values: What the consumers in a market value in their lives in general.

o Benefit: The benefits sought by the consumers in a market from the products they buy.

You're not going to use all of these variables at once. That will make your segments too narrowly focused. The scope of your segments must match your product. When your product is more expensive, customized, and specialized; it may need to be marketed to more focused and individualistic segments. Products that appeal to more people can be marketed to broader, more generalized segments.

The art of developing the best segments lies in finding the middle ground between too vague and too specific. Your unique business setup will require an equally unique segmentation strategy. It is up to you to find the right combination of bases and corresponding variables that will create adequate segments for your situation. You will know you're on the right track when you've created segments that are identifiable, measurable, substantial, accessible, and responsive.

Segmentation in Action

So, what does a viable segment look like? It will start with a geographic area that is large enough to house an adequate number of potential buyers. This pool is then divided by one or more demographic and/or usage rate variables, splitting it into various smaller segments. You can further define these segments with psychographic variables if you choose. The end result will be well-defined sections of the larger market.

Let 's explore an example: A men's barbershop owner services an area that spans a 50-mile radius from the shop's location. Residing within this area is 20,000 people, 12,000 of which are female, and 8,000 are male. Since the shop's service caters only to men, the 8,000 males in the service area would be the shop's marketing focus. The segmentation could end here because the shop offers a more generalized product (haircuts), a single marketing message can be used to solicit this entire population. The shop could also divide this male population further and create tailored messages to reach each segment individually. Add an age variable, split the population of males into 3 segments (ages 18-34, 35-50, and over 50), and now the focus is greatly intensified.

In this example, the barbershop has created 3 viable segments. They are identifiable by their gender and age. The segments are measurable because their population numbers can be acquired through the census. Although the numbers of the individual segments will vary, an overall market of 8,000 possible customers is substantial to a local barbershop. These segments are accessible because all can be reached with some type of advertising vehicle (television, radio, internet, print ads, Etc.). Finally, we can only assume that each of these segments will be responsive if the proper marketing messages are used.

Every segment within the entire market does not have to be identified either. Every person doesn't have to be classified. Instead, immediately eliminate those who are not likely to purchase your offering, then segment the remaining pool of potential customers. These are the consumers who deserve your marketing attention. These are the segments where most of your opportunities will be.

Select Your Target

Alright, you've narrowed down the market into only the segments relevant to your business. Somewhere within these segments is your target customer(s). Selecting your target customer is your task here. Pick one or more of the customer types that you've identified and aim your marketing efforts directly at them.

Your target market (customer) selection process will largely depend on your targeting strategy. As discussed earlier, a targeting strategy can be either undifferentiated (target the entire market at once), multi-segmented (target several smaller segments of the market at once), concentrated (target one specific niche of the market), or direct (target people on an individual level). Again, the type of product you sell will be indicative of what targeting strategy you should employ.

For many businesses, a multi-segment strategy makes the most sense. It still allows you the ability to speak directly to a certain segment alone. It offers you a chance to use different marketing messages and advertising vehicles to reach a variety of segments all at once, increasing your chance of success with at least one. It will usually be in your best interest to choose more than one target as long as it doesn't stretch your resources too thin while trying to reach them.

When selecting your targets, there are a few traits you should be looking for. One of the first is opportunity. Those segments that appear to have the most opportunity are choice. Opportunity can be found in a segment's spending power, purchase frequency, size, newness, and niche potential. Another positive trait is profitability. You want to target the most profitable customers with the lowest acquisition cost (overall cost of acquiring customer), highest propensity to become a returning customer, and most likely to pay base price for your products. The final trait to look for is receptiveness. The targets you choose should be receptive to the benefits your product offers them, but also able to identify with the image your company portrays.

Carefully choose your targets to the best of your ability. Use the criteria most important to you. Just be sure to pick the target customers who have the most potential. Once you have solidified your selections, record them in your marketing plan.

Profile Your Target

Now that your target has become clear, it is imperative that you complete a profile of each customer type. You need to collect as much personal in information about them as possible. This may require some additional research on your part, but it will be worth it because the more you know about them, the better your ability to communicate with them will be.

Your goal is to profile your targets as thoroughly as possible. You will be looking to gain a deeper understanding of who they are on a personal level. This information will be priceless in helping you develop messages that emphasize the benefits that your targets actually care about. And we all know that reaching them effectively is the first step towards a sale.

So, what's included in a profile? Whatever you feel is important! Any information that you can gather about the segments that you have chosen to target should be a part of their profile. You want to characterize them by analyzing their behaviors, values, point-of-view, desires, feelings, and attitudes. A complete profile will paint a vivid picture of a potential customer highlighting their unique qualities.

Describe Them

Profiling just means to describe. Jump into your target's shoes, describe "yourself", and "your" view of the world. Explain all those things that makes your target special. How does this person think? What is important to them? Why do they buy? What do they believe? What do they crave or desire? What do they fear? What do they love?

Other important information to add to your target customers profile:

- Purchase Behavior
- Expected Growth
- Brand Loyalty
- Profit Potential
- Size
- Brand Usage
- Sales Potential
- Influences

Remember those research skills you learned earlier? They will come in handy now. To complete adequate profiles of your target customers, you will have to study them and find out information about them. Some of their characteristics you may already know, but others you will have to learn through research. Be creative though in locating this information. Utilize the traditional research sources (data collecting organizations, government departments, interviews, test groups, etc.), but don't overlook new sources of consumer information like social media outlets, blogs, vlogs (video blogs), opinion forums, or photo posts. These can all give you some insight into the minds of your targets.

Describe your targets as accurately and as thoroughly as possible. Tell their story. Understand their life. Identify their character. This is how you create a profile that will be invaluable in helping you connect with your target customers.

Rank Them

If you choose to target several segments, you will find that they won't be all equally important. Some targets will prove to be more viable than others. Some will have more opportunity than others. Some will deserve more attention than others. For this reason, you should rank your target customers by importance.

> **For example**, if you have chosen four segments of the market to target, you could rank them number 1 to 4, highest to lowest. Number one would be the most important, and number four would be the least important. These will still be your targets, and you will be soliciting them all, but number one would be the highest priority and, and number four would be the lowest priority.

Your ranking system can also help you decide how to allocate your marketing resources. You may want to devote more of your attention and marketing budget to the higher ranked targets because they have the most potential. The lion's share of the budget may go to your top target while the others receive proportionately less marketing

Lastly, numbering your targets this way will make them easy to identify and recall. You can refer to each target by its designated number when discussing them with your marketing team. This helps to keep you organized when developing various communication initiatives to different targets.

Best Communication Methods

With your target market selected and profiled, you can determine what are the best ways to communicate with them. This is the main reason of targeting in the first place.

Each target customer will have certain communication methods and messages that they will respond to better than others. You need to use this information to decide which communication vehicles will most effectively reach them, as well as, which marketing messages will best speak to their interests.

It would be extremely difficult to communicate with a 21-year old African American male, and a 61-Year Old Asian female on a common level. They will have vastly different values with only a few commonalities; therefore, you will need to speak to each target on a platform that they will pay attention to, and a level that they can relate to personally. You may use radio ads to reach the young person, and newspaper ads to reach the older person, for example.

There is an appropriate communication method that will best reach any segment of the market. Just follow the profiles you created and analyze the types of media they like, the places they frequent, and the logic of their thinking. It will quickly become evident which communication method will yield the best results in reaching the segment. Write your ideas on the best communication methods for each target and include it as part of their profiles.

By now, you should be very familiar with your target market(s). You should be confident in your knowledge of who they are, what they care about, and how they operate. This knowledge will be useful in not only helping you communicate with them, but also providing them with total value.

∞

In the following chapter, we'll look at how you will translate target customer intelligence into a winning communication strategy. You will use all that you've learned about your targets to build highly customized marketing campaigns that are efficient at reaching these targets and getting results. Since amount of sales revenue will directly correlate with how well you can communicate with potential buyers, we must pay special attention to this next section. Let's keep on moving.

Chapter 8:
Marketing Plan Part Five:
Communication Plan

Try this experiment. Complete a profile of yourself. Record your demographic information, identify your characteristics, and label your personality traits. All of the measures you used before to profile is complete, then list all of the communication methods that you would best respond to.

Since you can profile yourself better than you can profile anyone else, this will be excellent practice for you. The point of this experiment is to give you an understanding of how profile information translates into a communication strategy. Based upon your personal information, it can be estimated that there are certain TV shows you watch, websites you visit, things you read, radio stations you listen to, places you drive, and other potential destinations where you can be reached. Also, based on your psyche, there are certain messages that will be more relevant to you than others. That's what this chapter is all about. Knowing your target and devising a plan to reach them.

This section represents the final "P" in the marketing mix-- promotion. The elements of promotion include advertising, sales promotion, and public relations. These elements are known as the promotion mix, and each of them has a special communicative use.

Even though you will use the promotional mix elements in different ways, they should blend together as integrated marketing communications. If done right, each element will be autonomous, but they will all coordinate to express a single main message. This is a key communication strategy because promotion is most effective as a campaign rather than as single messaging attempts.

After reading this chapter, you will understand how to develop a strong communication plan that is founded upon your promotional mix. You will discover various communication strategies that are designed to share your messages with the masses. Step-by-step you will put together a comprehensive plan that speaks to your targets in a variety of ways. Your first task will be to choose a primary message that is relevant to your targets interests. This message will serve as the theme or platform for your promotional campaign. Then, you must decide on which promotional vehicles you will use to convey the facts, figures, and benefits that support your campaign's main message. Finally, you will go into detail about how you intend to execute your strategy. If you follow these steps, you will form a great communications plan with the potential to deliver droves of customers to your businesses doorstep.

Designing Campaigns

The initial task in your communication planning is to design a promotional campaign with a well-defined theme. Campaigns are used to organize promotional initiatives keeping them uniform and consistent. The concepts for every promotion under a campaign will follow a pre-determined theme that you have developed. This theme will be the primary message that you think will best shape the public's perception's in your favor.

Themes

Think carefully about the theme of your campaign before deciding on it. Not only is your company's image and reputation on the line, but you don't want to waste resources investing into promotions with an ineffective messaging scheme. Your theme should be a more general message offering customers reasons why they should buy from you. "We have the" lowest prices, best customer service, highest quality, most stylish product, coolest company, best experience, or fastest delivery are all examples of possible campaign themes.

Promotional campaigns are supposed to keep all your communication efforts on track and on topic. It's easy to lose focus when you are using various types of promotional vehicles, your message could get lost in the shuffle. Avoid confusion and miscommunication with consistency and repetition of your campaign's theme in all of your promotions.

Communication Objectives

As you are designing your campaign, keep in mind your communication objective. When you communicate with consumers it is for one of three reasons: To inform, to persuade, or to remind. There is a specific strategy to each one of these objectives.

Informing messages are intended to tell people that you exist. New products or companies benefit from this objective because it gets the word out. When you are unknown, you have got to inform the public of who you are, what you offer, how it works, and other introductory specifics. Successful informative campaigns increase awareness of your company, an/or your new products.

Persuasive messages are used to convince people to act in some way. At this point, consumers are already aware of your offering, so now it's about persuading them to buy, try, call, visit, or prefer. Move than to some type of action. In persuading messages, the strategy is to tell the public about the advantages your product offers over the competitions. You will tout the attributes, benefits, and features of your product. A successful persuasive campaign will increase sales and market share because people will be buying more and possibly converting to your product.

Reminding messages are meant to refresh the public's memory about your product. When your product is in the mature stage of its life cycle, sometimes people need to be reminded that it is still on the market. A reminding campaign is considered to be a success when awareness of your product remerges, indicating that people's memory has been triggered.

Establishing an objective for each of your promotional campaigns makes them more effective. It is just another way to better focus your messages towards a common goal. When your product is new, your objective will be to inform the public that it exists. Once your product is known, the objective of your campaign will evolve, and the aim will be to persuade people to buy more of your product offering. After interest in your product has peaked, and you start to notice a decline in public attention, you will want to adopt a reminding message objective to tell them in new and fresh ways that your product still exists. Each objective has a specific purpose; keeping your messages aligned, this is where the value lies.

Message Clarity

Campaigns are designed to enhance the communication process. In any communication you have a sender, a receiver, and a message. The sender materializes ideas into meaning. The receiver accepts and interprets into meaning. Once the receiver acts on the message or provides feedback the communication cycle is complete. In this communication, your company is the sender, your targets are the receivers, and the theme of your campaign is the message. But how can you ensure that your message is received the way you intend it to be? If you don't want your messages to be interpreted incorrectly, you must be absolutely clear.

Before broadcasting any message to the public, you want to think about what it implies, the ways it could potentially be interpreted, and the affect it could have on the positioning of your product/brand. These are all major considerations that will lend clarity to your message and ensure that it comes across the right way. If not expressed correctly, value pricing can be construed as cheap, which is a term associated with low quality. In contrast, premium pricing can be seen as snooty and expensive, indicating that the product is overpriced and not worth it. You can't always control the interpretation, but the clearer you are, the better your messages will be received. By the time your message reaches the receiver you want its meaning to be intact.

Speaking of the receiver, another consideration that will add clarity to your messages is your target audience's characteristics. How is the particular target most likely to interpret the message you are sending? Something that one target may find funny, another may find offensive. This is why before crafting any promotions you must know who you are communicating with. The main message may be the same, but the way to deliver it should depend on the audience.

Supporting the Theme

The theme of your campaign is the main message that you want to share with the public, but there are a variety of ways for you to express it. Your promotions will use different creative concepts and sub--messages to support your campaigns theme. Each promotion that your marketing department uses should build upon the campaign's theme in its own way.

There are many concepts that can be derived from a campaign's general message. Let's say, for instance, that the theme of one of your campaigns pertains to the durability of your product. A sales promotion that will support this message could be a demonstration that allows consumers to test the strength of the product. Then, a supporting advertisement could be created that shows scenes of consumers trying unsuccessfully to damage the product. Lastly, a public relations press release could be written that explains the ground-breaking manufacturing process your company uses to make such a durable product. Each of these different promotion types lend credibility to your campaign's main claim. Their concepts support the theme by showing how and why your product is so durable.

You should never have an advertisement, sales promotion, or self-initiated public relation interaction that deviates from the theme of the campaign that governs it. Use the theme that you have developed as a basis when brainstorming any promotional ideas. If you come across a good concept but the message doesn't support the campaign you are working on, put it to the side and use it on another campaign where it will be relevant. This is the best way to focus your messages, so they have the greatest impact and achieve optimal results.

Using the AIDA Model

"Buy my product" is the underlying message that guides all of your promotional campaigns. Getting potential buyers to the point where they are ready to actually make a purchase is the overall objective here. The ADIA model is a concept that explains how to use communication to move consumers along this line. It is based on human thinking patterns. The acronym stands for **A**ttention, **I**nterest, **D**esire, and **A**ction.

Each portion of the AIDA concept is a stage. The first stage is to get the attention of the target. Second, you begin to build their interest in the message. In the third stage, the target develops a desire for what you are offering. Finally, if the communication is effective, the target will take action.

The AIDA concept has been used for years by marketing professionals to help them craft the most effective marketing messages. If you are doing your own promotions, you can use this concept just as well. All you need is a better understanding of the elements.

Attention

To begin communicating you must grab the attention of the targets. In today's oversaturated marketing environment this is becoming increasingly difficult. There are so many other entities vying for the attention of all the same people, and this creates a high level of "noise" which can distort your messages. Breaking through this noise is by far the biggest challenge.

Creativity will be your greatest asset when you are trying to command the attention of an audience. You need to find a way to stand out from the pack to really get noticed. This can be achieved with publicity stunts, cutting edge advertisements, grand sales promotions, or any other creative and original promotional activity. Even the unique features of your product may get you noticed. There are many ways to earn the attention of a target; however, this attention span will be short so when you get it you must act quickly to insert your message and begin building interest.

Interest

In this second stage, your aim is to gain the interest of your targets. You've secured their attention, but only briefly. To keep them focused on the communication, you must get them interested in your message and your product offering. This is done by showing off your product. Put it in front of the public's eyes and tell them about it.

The key here is to give your targets just enough to keep them waiting to know more. If you tease them with bits of information at a time, their level of interest will build, and they will seek additional supplementary information about your good or service. Use sales promotions like exhibitions or advertisements to show off the attributes and features of your offering. The more you can educate customer prospects about what you are selling. The more interested they will be in it.

Desire

Desire is created once you show consumers why they should buy your product. You have to give them a reason to value what you are selling. This means successfully transforming the features that you expressed before, into benefits that will be relevant to your targets.

In this context, features can be defined as the desirable traits that your product offers. How these traits can be used to enrich the lives of consumers are benefits. Translate features into benefits, and consumers interest evolves into genuine desire.

Another way to build desire is to express the competitive advantages that your company holds, this is the time to brag about them. Convince consumers that your product deserves to be recognized as better. Once your goods or services are perceived as the preferable choice in the market, consumers will desire them.

Action

The final step in the model is the culmination of all your work in the other steps. It is the pay off. This is where you get the targets to actually do what you what them to do--spend their money with you. In advertising jargon, its known as the "call to action". All you have to do is tell people how, and where to get your product. That's it! If you were effective in the other elements of AIDA, then consumers will be rushing to take action and become your customers.

Applying AIDA

The elements of AIDA can be executed separately using different promotions, or all condensed into each promotional vehicle. Those with larger marketing budgets and bigger promotional campaigns can afford to focus on one AIDA element at a time and use a variety of promotions to move consumers from few promotions, then each promotion type will need to include all the elements of AIDA together so that you can move consumers to action with less exposure. Both ways can be equally effective if applied correctly.

For most small business owners, we need to get the most "bang" for every marketing buck. We need to squeeze every drop of utility out of all our communications. For this reason, it is suggested that you move through the entire AIDA progression in any promotion that you produce. If you were to place an AD in a magazine for instance, that AD may be a huge chunk of your marketing budget, so it has to grab attention, build interest, create desire, and call for action all at once. This can be done if you take the time to be creative and pragmatic.

Promotion Mix

How are you going to communicate with target customer's? What promotional vehicles will you use to reach them? These are the fundamental challenges that your communications plan must address. Here is where you will develop your promotional mix. You will choose the promotion types that will be used to conduct your marketing campaign(s).

To recap, a promotional mix can include any combination of advertising, public relations, and sales promotion initiatives. In building your promotional mix, you have to decide how you will put these promotion types to work delivering your campaign's themes. For each type, you will develop concepts to effectively express your marketing messages to the public. The promotional mix you end up with is what you will use to meet your communication objectives.

Each tool of a promotional mix has a specific identity with unique qualities. Each has an inherent usage value when it comes to communicating with customer prospects. Advertising reaches people in a way that public relations and sales promotions cannot. Sales promotions express value better than public relations and advertising. Public relations have a way of building consumer trust unlike any sales promotions or advertisements. All the promotion types have certain nuances and communicating abilities. To best utilize these tools, you have to know more about them.

Public Relations

Also known as PR, public relations are unpaid communications opportunities. PR messages are shared with the public through news and other outlets. The intent is to educate and shape the perceptions of the public about your product or company. The idea is to plan activities that will enhance your organization's image and minimize anything that can produce a negative image. PR is a valuable tool and a necessary part of any promotional mix.

The actual function of public relations is to manage your firm's relationship with the public. This is done primarily using news outlets. People tend to trust the news media more than any other source of information, so this can definitely be used to your advantage if you know how to harness it's power.

Getting the media's attention is the key, you need publicity. You can earn this publicity with press releases, internet videos, interviews, press events, and so forth. If you can generate newsworthy situations, the news media will follow. Remember their product is news so they need your news stories just as much as you need the publicity.

Public Relations comes in many forms. Some of the most commonly used are:

- **Press Releases** - These are articles written by your organization that cover newsworthy stories about your product, your particular company, or the industry you're in. Press releases should not look like advertisements, they should be actual news stories that casually mention the name of your products, or your company within them. Once you have an adequate article, you then release it to various news media outlets with the hopes that several of them will publish an exact copy, or at least, a reproduction of it as news. Be sure that you include the name of your company, your web address, and the number where you can be reached in the article.

> **Example** - A carpet cleaning company could release an article that informs people about the health hazards related to dirty carpets. The owner of the company could give his "expert opinion" in the article telling readers that the best way to stay safe is to have the carpet professionally cleaned every six months. This provides the opportunity to place the name and contact information of his service in the article. In this press release, the carpet cleaning company states a problem, then provides a solution.

- **Press Events** - When you have some big news to share with the public (like a new product, new location opening, or an ownership change) you can schedule a press event to get the word out. The event can be a news conference, a ribbon cutting, a ground breaking, or any other type of event. Inform the media by sending out press kits. A press kit includes a full explanation of the event, who is involved, the location, the date/time of the event, press releases about the event, and anything else you find important.

Example - A new company that is just opening for business could host grand opening ceremony and invite all the press to be present.

- **Interviews** - Meeting with the press where you answer a series of questions about your product, company, or a particular topic relevant to your business. Can be conducted on television, radio, magazine, online, or newspaper. Being interviewed usually makes your company look like highly capable experts who can be trusted to serve the public.

Example - The owner of a retail store could give an interview about how her business is preparing to accommodate the expected increaser of customers for the "Black Friday" shopping day.

- **Sponsorships** - When there is an event that your company wishes to be aligned or affiliated with, you can donate resources to assist with the planning of that event. In return, the event organizers will announce your company as a sponsor of the event. The organizers can acknowledge your sponsorship in a variety of ways like: Placing your name and logo on banners, signs, t-shirts, or programs dispersed throughout the event; mentioning your company as a sponsor before the event and during the event; or offering representatives from your company an opportunity to attend the event to promote your business.

Example - A manufacturer of tires would be inclined to sponsor any popular racing event. Cost of sponsorship could be actual cash, or they could provide the tires for vehicles participating in the race for free.

- **Product Placement** - Having your product appear in a work of art (movies, video games, books, television shows, etc.) as itself. This lends realism and authenticity to the artwork (especially when your product already has some brand recognition) while offering exposure of your brand to the audience of the art work must be similar to your target audience for the product placement to be useful.

> **Example** – A new clothing designer persuades a popular recording artist to wear the clothes in a music video and mention the brand name in a song.

- **Charity** - There are many ways to apply the public relations tactic. You can plan and/or sponsor charity events, donate funds to a particular charity, or you can even set up your own charity in the name of your company. This builds goodwill with the public because it shows that you care about more than just making profits. It shows that you are willing to give back to the community that you serve.

> **Example** - A company can set up a program where they pledge to donate a certain amount of their proceeds, for a certain time, to a charity of their choosing. This allows the customer a chance to also feel like they are contributing to a cause while showing the company's compliment to the cause as well.

- **Internet Videos** - Creating videos, to be posted online, using concepts that pertain to your business in some way. These videos can be funny or serious, informative or abstract, specific or vague. The goal is to create a video that goes "viral". Video that gets a large number of views in a relatively short amount of time is considered viral. There's no formula for creating a viral video because today's internet viewer has hyper-dynamic preferences that change all the time. No matter what the video is about, the best policy is to make them interesting.

Example – An auto mechanic shop can put together an internet video showing people tips on how to change a flat tire. Or the shop could make a video attempting the "world's fastest oil change". Both types of videos have the potential to become viral, but also shows the company's professionalism and builds videos the shop would be sure to give their name, number, an ID website in a creative way as well.

- **Blogging** – An internet platform where you can write journal entries about different topic. Even though this is less popular than it used to be, it is still relevant. Blogging perpetuates your image as an expert in the field. The topic that you are blogging about must be interesting and relevant to your business in some way. You can write blogs on your own website, and/or on site set up specifically for blogging.

Example - A touring company may set up a blog about the different events that are going on in their service area (parties, festivals, art shows, concerts, etc.). This would show that they are knowledgeable of all the hottest location and events.

- **Social Media Pages** - Creating company profiles on social media websites where you can interact with the public. The most popular social media sites currently are Facebook, Twitter, Instagram, and snapchat. There is a plethora of other sites though that cater to many different interests and demographics types. This is an excellent way to directly communicate with potential customers. Also, by paying attention to posts, an opportunity is created to gather information on your target's likes, dislikes, activities, and mindsets.

> **Example** - A food truck business sets up a Facebook account and builds a following of people who like their food. The company can then post messages to all their Facebook "friends" letting 'them know where the truck will be located for the day serving people. In order for the company's page to not appear like only an advertisement, they would need to also post informative type messages about topics like cooking tips, upcoming events, or local news stories for example.

Advertising

Advertising is the most commonly used and well understood type of promotional vehicle. Basically, advertisements are paid-for platforms upon which marketing messages are delivered to the public. unlike public relations, there is a clear understanding that advertising messages are created by companies specifically for the purpose of advancing positions, altering perceptions, or persuading people to buy. In other words, consumers are well aware that they are being solicited to when they see an ad.

Advertising offers marketers a high level of control in conveying messages. Whatever you want to communicate can be relayed most directly, because the audience understands that solicitation is what this platform is all about.

No cloaking devices needed. You don't have to hide the message, or mindset. Just find creative ways to tell consumers "buy my products" or "my products are the best because... " or "my prices are the lowest..." or any other marketing message. Be straightforward but artful. Any advertisement can be classified as one of two types: Brand advertising or direct advertising. There are some distinct and notable differences between the two. There is a specific application for each. The differences are based upon usage.

Brand advertising is designed with the intention of building brand awareness and preference among a target audience. It is not meant to sell by itself, but to be part of a larger effort to create familiarity so that when consumers see the brand at a retail location they choose it over others.

Because brand advertisements require a high level of repetition to be effective, the cost of this strategy is high. Many times the only types of organizations that can afford to engage in brand advertising are those with larger marketing budgets. It is a huge investment, and the return is not always immediate, but the brand recognition and familiarity that is built as a result is highly valuable if the product is made available on a wide scale.

You will know a branding type advertisement when you see it because it will be missing the obvious "buy now" call to action. They won't directly ask for a purchase, or call, or visit. The focus will only be on enhancing the brand's image. The objective of brand advertising is simply to make consumer's view an organization and its products more favorably.

In contrast, direct advertising urges audiences to act in some way. These advertisements directly ask consumers to purchase a product, call for more information, visit a website, or stop in to the business. Repetition is less necessary here because direct advertisements look to close a sale immediately. Each ad is a complete sales pitch within itself, with the hope that fewer ads will be needed to illicit action.

Direct advertising is usually the best option for small businesses. Primarily because most times they don't have an abundance of resources to spend on promotion. Each of the advertisements that small business produce needs to have to potential to move consumers from product introduction to product sale in one swift move. It is rare for any single promotion to have this kind of power, but this is the mindset needed to create the best direct advertisements.

Any direct advertisement, no matter the concept, has three parts. The first part, called the offer, explains to the audience what the advertisement is offering. It sells the product 's features by expressing than as benefits that the target audience can relate to. For example, a product with enhanced safety features offers consumers a piece of mind and a protected feeling as benefits.

The second part of a direct advertisement is the call to action. This is where the audience is told exactly what the advertiser wants them to do. Usually, this will mean asking them to purchase, or at least, make an inquiry so that they can be sold to personally. Sample call to action statements are ' 'get yours today", "act now", "call NOW for more information", "Get a free quote", and so forth.

The final component in direct advertisements, the response device, provides the audiences with a way to respond to the ad. After asking people to act in sane way, they have to be informed on how to act. This is where a phone number, or website, or business location is provided where the audience can respond to the advertisement and take advantage of the offer.

Direct advertisements and brand advertisements alike normally involve what is known as a USP (unique selling proposition). This is the exclusive and desirable benefit that your product offers that none other can match. A USP canes in the form of a simple statement that explains why your product is unique. Maybe your products are hard--crafted by a world--renowned artisan, or your product can teach a person to speak a second language in only 90 days guaranteed, these are both viable USPs. Many times, a USP is translated into sane type of slogan or in advertisements. 'I'm loving it", "Have it your way", "Eat fresh", sound familiar? These are past USPs for McDonalds, Burger' King, and Subway respectively.

Advertisements deliver messages using print, internet, or broadcast media platforms. Each of these platforms have a variety of vehicles to express messages.

Print Advertisements are singular and static solicitations. They use a visually graphic element, as well as a text element, to convey messages. Print advertisements can appear anywhere in various forms including:

- Periodical (magazine, newspaper, Etc.)
- Billboard
- Flyer
- Brochures
- Leaflet/pamphlet
- In-store display
- Signs
- Benches
- Transit (Bus, Taxi, truck, Etc.)
- Posters
- Classifieds
- And many others...

Internet Advertisements are those that exist exclusivity on an internet platform. Internet ads can come in the form of simple text formats, audio, video, others, the capability of this platform is wide ranged, with few limits. The cost can be low, but has the potential to skyrocket as well. Also, the platform has the ability to reach millions of people. There are various ways to utilize the internet for advertising purposes including:

- Banner Ads (Static or Rich Media)
- Pay Per Click Links (Google ad words)
- Online Classifieds
- Pop-up Ads
- Podcasts
- E-mail
- "App" Ads

- Contextual Ads
- Game Creation
- Webisodes (Short movies that promote brands)
- Inbound Links
- QR Codes

Broadcast Advertisements are more dynamic in nature with moving sights and/or sounds. They are broadcast to thousands, up to millions, of potential customers at a time. They are presented in short increments with strict time constraints and tend to be the most expensive advertisement type. These ads reach customer using:

Television

- Cable
- Local Stations
- Infomercial

Radio

- National Stations
- Local Stations
- Satellite Radio

Sales Promotion

Sales promotion encompasses all those communication activities not considered as advertising or public relations. They are meant to affect consumer purchasing behavior by offering desirable incentives. Using discounts, rebates, coupons, and other draws; sales promotions lure targets into sales opportunities.

The most effective sales promotions present offers that can't be refused--deals that are too good to pass by. A quality discount promotion will make those who act on it feel like they got an exceptional value, while making those who don't act regret it sharply. It should reward people for becoming customers.

Discounting is not the only form of sales promotion though. Other forms are more hands on and requires dealing with target customers on a one-to-one level. Initiatives like trade shows, demos, or sampling, puts a company in direct contact with the public in an attempt to build relationships. Being in such close proximity to consumers creates great opportunities to persuade them to buy and makes it easier to measure the success of the activities.

Sales promotion is less expensive than most forms of advertising. The monthly budget for a local television advertising campaign can easily reach $20, 000 or more. Radio spots, on average, can be $6,000 per month. In contrast, a sales promotion that is based on offering discounts only costs after a sale is made; a campaign to distribute samples is relatively cheap; and setting up a booth at a trade show usually requires only minimal resources. In most cases, sales promotions themselves are low cost, but you must get the word out. This is why sales promotion and advertising will forever be married. Informing people of an existing sales promotion requires some level of advertising, so they go hand-in-hand.

Sales promotions come in a wide variety of forms. The only limit is your imagination. Some well-known examples are:

- Coupons Rebates
- Premiums
- Discounts
- Store Displays Loyalty Programs
- Trade Show Set-ups
- Demonstrations o Samples

- Giveaways
- Sweepstakes
- Contests
- Games

Integrating Promotional Elements

The elements you use to construct your promotional with are the most effective when they work together. Even though they are all different, and each element has a specific use, they must all coordinate seamlessly to communicate uniform marketing messages. Ideally, they will work together towards achieving the same goal, while maintaining your company's desired image.

The theme of your campaign will be the com-on factor that ties together your promotional activities. Every concept that you employ should promote the main idea of your campaign. For instance, an informative campaign that focuses on the customization feature of a new headwear product line can be expressed in a few different ways. First, a print advertisement could be designed that explains how the headwear products can be customized to the consumer's exact specifications. Then, a public relations internet video could be released that portrays the creative ways that current customers are customizing their hats. Last, as a sales promotion, a contest Can be held where customers upload their own pictures of their customized hats to the company's website. Those voted by the public as most creative win prizes. Each of these promotions tie—in together to support the campaign's theme of customization ability.

Integrating your promotional mix elements, and their corresponding messages, is simply a matter of following your campaign themes. Each concept you develop for any promotional medium should strictly adhere to the theme at hand. This is how the marketing professionals do it. If the idea deviates from the primary message, it shouldn't be used.

Let's say that you decide to hire a publicist, an advertising firm, and a sales promotion consultant to handle your promotion mix. How will you coordinate their efforts? How will you make sure that the message among the three entities remains uniform? To achieve this kind of cohesion and consistency, you have to make sure that these contractors are aware of the common campaign theme in play at the time. If the primary

campaign message is used to govern the promotional ideas of each contractor, their separate activities should automatically line up with one another. This stands true even if you are doing your own public relations, advertising, and sales promotion work. Integrate the three under the umbrella of common campaign themes.

Building a favorable image for your product in the minds of consumers takes time and steady exposure. Shaping people's perceptions requires repetition and untimely. Strive to be seen as much as possible, in as many places as possible, using as many platforms as possible. Adequately integrate your promotional mix elements, and every time you are exposed to the public, you will be promoting a consistent message that establishes your company's unique identity. This is the point of developing a communications plan.

Other Promotional Mix Considerations

When deciding which promotional mix elements to use, and how to use them, there are sane additional variables that you should consider first.

Overall Cost

Every promotional activity, except good old-fashioned word-of-mouth, has some sort of attached cost. Some cost more than others, like television ads which have some of the highest overall costs, and others are less expensive, like press releases, which have almost no cost. Overall cost accounts for all the expenses associated with providing the promotion including: set—ups, creation, publishing, and others. The overall cost will be a big factor in your choice of promotional mediums because you have to be able to afford the investment.

Cost Per Contact

Cost per contact measures the cost of an advertising space relative to the number of people it is projected to reach. To formulate cost per contact, you divide the cost of publishing an advertisement (print, broadcast, internet) by the estimated number of people who will be exposed to it. This measures reveals a different outlook which sometimes puts an overall cost into perspective. Television ads, which sometimes puts overall cost into perspective.

Television ads, which has a very high overall cost, also has a wide reach, making the cost per contact very low. If you paid $20,000 for a television spot that reaches 1,000,000 people, then your cost per contact is only $0.02. This means that your company is paying only 2 cents for each exposure to a potential customer. Knowing this, now it seems a little more economical and worth it doesn't it?

[Cost of advertising space / Number of people it will reach = CPC]

Even though cost per contact is primarily used to measure advertising mediums, it can be applied to other promotional types as well. You can take the overall cost of other mediums and divide that among the number of people you project it will reach, and you will get a type of cost per contact. Use this measure to better assess the worth of a promotional activity prior to engaging in it.

Reach

How many consumers will be exposed to a promotion constitutes its reach. A press release news story that appears in a national magazine has more reach than one in a local newspaper. The circulation (number of people subscribed to the publication) for a national magazine will most likely be higher than that of the local newspaper. But, it is more difficult to get your story in the national magazine than in the local paper. Similarly advertising in the national magazine will be more expensive. The point is, more reach usually means more resources will be required.

Before adding a communication form to your promotion mix be sure that it has adequate reach for your purposes. Depending on the response rate (the rate upon which people act on a promotion) you will need to reach a significant number of people in order to maintain consistent business and cash flow. Of course, you want to reach as many targets as possible, but what does your budget allow? Choose the promotional activities that give you the most reach for the smallest investment.

Frequency

Repetition builds memory. Repetition creates familiarity. Repetition feeds desire. Eventually, repetition will lead to action. The frequency of a promotion has a direct effect on its ability to initiate consumer purchasing behaviors. The more effective it will be.

Certain promotional mediums naturally have high frequency potential. Billboard are viewed by people who drive past them on their way to work every day.

Promotional gift items that don your logo (like refrigerator magnets, mouse pads, or desk calendars) remind people of your company on a consistent basis without them realizing it. A good publicity stunt caught on video, could be replayed on various news outlets as well as posted to the internet, which could expose it to people several times during its run.

As you are putting together your promotional mix think about how you can maximize frequency among the elements you choose. You want each promotional activity to have a good level of frequency on its own, but you also want them to coordinate together to provide repetitiveness as well. The elements need to complement each other in a way that maximizes the chance that a single target could be exposed to them all. In a well—oiled promotional mix, a consumer will see a product in an advertisement, read about it in the newspaper, and be persuaded to buy it because of a sales promotion.

Audience Selectivity

Another important consideration is audience selectivity. This is the ability of a promotional medium to reach a precisely defined market. Years ago it was difficult to reach a specific audience; today, it is possible to reach audiences down to the most detailed characteristics. In fact, the trend has been moving toward more closely defined target markets than general ones. With this being said, you want the promotions you use to offer the greatest amount of selectivity, or the most narrowly defined audience.

A great contemporary example of this is the current cable television advertising system. Many cable companies, because of the digital format, now have the capability to segment their audiences on a geographic basis. This offers advertising the opportunity to select specifically which areas they would like to target with their ads. each program already has a certain demographic that it reaches, but the cable companies take this a step further by also selling ad space on a zip code basis. This vastly improves the selectivity of the medium and allows for pinpoint accuracy in reaching specific targets. Further, this system has made television advertising economical and available to smaller companies who normally couldn't afford it. Instead of advertisements being sold in huge expensive national or regional reaching blocks, they can also be sold in miniature local blocks that have less reach but are more affordable.

The better the audience selectivity of a medium, the less waste that is accumulated. Every person that your promotion reaches, who is not classified as a target, is considered a waste. You don't want to waste resources trying to reach people who have little to no potential of becoming one of your customers. You've spent the time to closely define your targets; therefore, it would behoove you to choose the promotional types that have an adequate amount of audience selectivity to suit your needs. This way, you can ensure that you reach them and no one else.

Communication Strategy

If you want your attempts at communication to be absorbed by your targets, your strategy will be coherence through coordination. Coordinate your communication efforts to present clear messages. Ensure that your messages are received and interpreted correctly by keeping them consistent. Each one of your promotional activities should be working towards improving your position and ultimately selling your product offering.

Another objective of your communication strategy is solidifying your image, building your brand. With effective communication, you Can print whatever picture of your business that you want to portray. As your company's desired image becomes entrenched in the minds of cŒ1surners, you will earn their trust and respect. As your brand builds strength and recognition, it gains intrinsic value. Once you create a favorable perception of your product offering, persuading people to buy is much easier and less costly.

Use the intelligence that you have collected on your target 's to determine which promotional vehicles will best reach them. Strategize on how you can most effectively deliver your messages at the right time, without being intrusive. When you are developing your communication plan, just think of yourself from the perspective of your target. What would grab your attention? What would persuade you to make a purchase?

Your communication strategy should squeeze every inch of utility out of your promotional budget. You are looking to get as much exposure as possible from every dollar that you invest in marketing communication in the perfect strategy, your messages are clear and consistent, your company is continuously in view of the public, your brand gets enhanced, and your money is spent most efficiently. The result? flood of new customer's sales revenues.

Writing the Communication Plan

Of all the sections your marketing plan contains, this o probably deserves the most attention. Devote the time to complete your communication plan by first materializing your ideas, organizing them into a scheme. The vision you had of how you wanted to promote your business should come to fruition here.

Start writing your communication plan focusing on developing campaign themes. You can choose to run one campaign at a time, or several at once. This will depend on your strategy and the position(s) that you are trying to accomplish. Regardless of how many campaigns you decide run concurrently, just ensure that each of their primary messages are designed to improve the public's perception of your company and/or convince them to buy.

Once you have come to a conclusion on the campaign themes that suit your needs, you can then begin writing down all your ideas of the promotional types, and corresponding concepts, that you want to use to deliver these messages. This is the fun part! Designing promotional mixes that will effectively execute your marketing campaigns gets your creative juices flowing and makes you excited about selling your products.

In your communication plan, write down what promotional vehicles you plan to use, and how you plan to use them. If you decided that you are going to print advertisements in a regional newspaper for example, then also write ideas for what the ads might look like and how they might read. As you are doing this, keep in consideration the tone of your concepts. Tone of voice can be indicative of your organization's promotional style. When your promotional concepts have either an edgy; witty; serious; funny; or quirky feel, this will represent your company's unique way of promoting its products. Following a promotional style in this way will help to build the identity of your company/brand.

No communication plan can be complete until each proposed promotional campaign has its own promotional mix. There should be at least one public relations, sales promotions, and advertising initiative for each campaign. Remember, the only way for your messages to be effectively communicated is for the promotional mix elements to integrate and work together. Plan to utilize every promotional mix element, instead of just one or two. This is how you get the best results.

The communication plan you end up with should be comprehensive and well-developed. At this point you should have various ideas of promotional tools that you want to utilize for your business. You may not use all of them but having them on paper will help you decide which ones will best deliver your campaign messages while remaining within your budget.

∞

The company that best expresses its marketing messages will take a lead in the continuous battle for market share. But this is only one aspect of competition; it goes much deeper. In the following chapter, we'll discuss competition further and find out what it takes to stay ahead.

Chapter 9:
Marketing Plan Part Six
Competition

The marketing war is underway and now that you have charted the landscape (market analysis) you are ready to battle for position. Who are you fighting though? How many of them are out there? How big are they? What type of weapons do they have? You have to know your enemy if you want to defeat your enemy. You must understand your competition.

Successful business owners are also fierce competitors. You should develop this same mindset if you want to become a market conquering entrepreneur. To stay one step ahead of your competitors you need to study them, understand them, and get to know them well. This intelligence will help you to anticipate their moves, and then plan your counters.

Before you are done reading this chapter you will learn the art of competitive intelligence. All of the techniques included here will teach you how to first identify, then evaluate your opponents. The aim is to create a working profile of each competitor that can be used later to create a comprehensive competitive strategy.

Who are Your Competitors?

In the previous chapter you made a list of all your perceived direct and indirect competitors. You also gave each of the direct competitors a threat level assessment score of 1 to 5. Now, in this section of the marketing plan, you will need to build a profile for each of you top 2-3 most critical opponents. Acknowledging that they exist is not enough, you need to get more personal; you need to know exactly who they are.

Location

Begin your first profile by listing the name and location of your most threatening competitor. Include the proximity of the opponent is to your business. For many companies, competition intensifies with competitors who are closest to them. Walk-up customer, for example, will have a direct choice between one business or the other especially when the businesses are next door or across the street from each other.

Be sure to describe the unique features of their physical location in the profile. Pay close attention to the ambience and theme. Assume that everything is designed strategically, because it probably is. What does it look like one that be outside/inside? What type of atmosphere have they created? What kind of vibe do you get when you enter? This will give you a good comparison for your own storefront. You'll be able to see if your location is up to par or if you need to upgrade.

Key Players

If possible, but a face on your competitors by identifying the key players within their organization. This includes owners, board members, directors, officers, managers, and any other VIP of their company. You don't need to be too specific, but briefly describe their title, what they do for the company, and anything else you may know about them (specialties, personality traits, tendencies).

Any information that you can collect on your competitor's key players is valuable competitive intelligence. These are the actual people that you will be competing against; the shot callers and decision makers. Their collective abilities will be reflective of the company's capabilities as a whole. Understanding the key players on a personal level is a definite advantage.

Philosophy/Vision

If you can, try to decipher your competitor's overall philosophy as part of their profile. Find out what they believe in, what is important to them, and why they are in business. This is a clue to your competitors thought processes and their perception of the world. Any decision they make, and strategy they employ will be based upon their philosophy. Your competitors will be looking to fulfill their vision. Knowing this vision will prove helpful in anticipating their strategies.

Additional Info.

Profile with any additional armored units may have collected about editors I can never have too much, and there's no bad intelligence and fat except in accurate intelligence. Any bit of information you find that you think may be useful add it, because they can only help your profile.

Research Their Operation

You don't really know your competitors until you explore all aspects of their operation. You need to know what they are selling in how they are selling it. You want to be aware of their marketing techniques. Your objective is to understand the particulars of their business.

Finding Competitive Intelligence

So, how do you find competitive intelligence? You could hire a C.I.A. trained espionage specialist to do some spying for you, but this will be expensive though. If you can't afford that, you will have to do your own dirty work. It sounds difficult, but if you know what to look for, and where to find it, you can gather your own competitive intelligence just as good as a professional spy.

The number one way to collect information about your competitors is to visit their business. Go to their premises and observe the environment. Look at the design and setup of their sales floor. What catches your eye? Where is everything located? How do they display their products? Note observances about their employees as well. Pay special attention to the customer service that you received during your visit. To get the best information, be hypersensitive to everything that is going on around you while you're at your competitor's place of business. Make a mental note of what you see, then later, record them on paper.

If your competitor has a web site, take the time to review it as part of your research. This is an excellent source of competitive intelligence. On many web sites you can find information about a company's management team, philosophy, culture, products, hours of operation, prices, and sometimes even their annual report (if the company is publicly traded). Look for any specials or promotion that they may be running as well because these are subtle clues to their marketing strategy among other things. There is a wealth of company data that is revealed within an online presence, that is why you should "tap this well".

Observe your competitor's virtual storefront in the same fashion that you observed their "brick-and-mortar" storefront. Take note of how professional it looks and its functionality. What features does it have? How user friendly is it? Use their site as a comparison to see how your own insight stacks up, and if you find some good ideas don't be ashamed to use them in your own way. This is a completely ethical practice.

Analyze the Competitors' Product

Once you purchase your competitors' products analyze it completely. You need to learn as much about it as possible. Everything from its utility down to the way it has been engineered. Compare it to your product offering to find out how similar or different it is.

When analyzing the competitor's product pay attention to:

- **Packaging**
  - o What is it made of?
  - o What message does it emphasize?
  - o Is unique?
  - o Does this serve a purpose besides just packaging?

- **Attributes of the product**
  - o Ingredients
  - o Texture
  - o Smell
  - o Shape
  - o Color
  - o Sounds
  - o Quality
  - o Craftsmanship
  - o Durability

- **Function of the Product**
  - o What is it used for?
  - o How does it work?

- o How well does it work?

- o How easy is it to use?

- o Does it have more than one use?

- **Manufacture**

  - o What is it made from?

  - o How well is it constructed?

When you are testing their product think like a consumer would. Break it down to its basics, understand it on an elemental level. Point out the good things about their product, but more importantly, highlight its flaws. Find out where it is most vulnerable and use this as your point of attack.

Size Them Up

Your next task is to estimate the dimensions of your competitors. You are trying to figure out how big they are. To achieve this, you will measure their size in terms of employees, customer base, sales volume (in units), revenues, and market share. Finding this information will be crucial in assessing the threat of each competitor.

The number of people that a competitor employs is an indication of their size. Most likely, the more employees they have, the more they are selling. When you visit their business look at how big the building is, how many cars are in the parking lot, and how many employees you actually see. You will have a problem with this if your competitor operates exclusively online and it doesn't have a physical location. In that situation, your estimate will be more rough. In either case, just give the best guess that you can as to how many employees your competitor has.

Finding out how many customers your competitors are serving can be challenging, but this figure will provide a strong basis for estimating the other measures. The best way to develop an estimate for this number is to perform a stakeout. Spend an hour, on an average business day, surveilling their premises to see how many customers come and go. Multiply this number by the number of hours their businesses open in a week to get a decent estimate of their average weekly customer traffic. Granted, this is time consuming and can be considered extreme, but it will get the job done.

For web-based competitors you need another method. Since you can't physically see the transactions, you must be a bit craftier to locate this information. The biggest clue will be web site traffic. One way to find this is to check how high the competitors web sites appear in Google search results. When you type in the different keywords that relate to your industry into the Google search bar, see where your competitors web sites are listed in the results. The higher they are listed the more trusting they are likely to have. It will be safe to assume that the competitors with high amounts of traffic are likely selling well online. Give your best estimate as to how many customers they are serving online using whatever information that you can find out about their web site traffic.

It is important to point out that these numbers will not necessarily be exact, nor do they have to be. You are only trying to get somewhere "in the ballpark" when estimating your competitor's customer base. Your goal is to create some usable benchmarks. No matter how you choose to estimate the number of customers that your competitors are serving, just to be sure that your method is based in some type of competitive knowledge.

Estimating the Size of Your Competitor's Business

Competitor's Avg. # of Customers Served per Week	X	Avg. # of Units Sold per Customer	=	Est. Unit Sales Volume
Competitor's Est. Unit Sales Volume	X	Unit Price	=	Est. Weekly Revenues
Competitor's Yearly Estimated Units Sold	X	Est. Yearly Units Sold in the Entire Market	=	Est. Unit Market Share
Competitor's Yearly Estimated Revenues	X	Total Yearly Value (in $) for the Entire Market	=	Est. Revenue Market Share

So far you have developed a good guess for the number of customers that you believe your competitor serves. At this point you can use this figure to estimate their unit sales volume, revenues, and market share. These are all relatively simple calculations to make now that you have a base.

Estimating these measures will shine a light on the size of your competitors. Those shown to have higher sales, revenues, and market share will naturally demand more of a competitive focus from you. The information that you have collected here will help you assess what you are up against with each competitor and how much ground you must cover to compete effectively.

How They Sell Their Offerings

Another important piece of competitive intelligence is figuring out how your competitors are selling their products. Those firms with higher sales are doing something right, and those with lower sales are lacking somewhere. Either way, you can gain great knowledge of what works and what doesn't.

Search for your competitor's promotional methods everywhere. Find fliers, billboards, TV/radio commercials, print ads, Internet ads, and any other type of promotional material that they release. What advertising vehicles are they using? What message are they communicating? How are they communicating this message?

What image do they portray in the minds of consumers?

In addition to the competitors chosen advertisement vehicles you should also note any sales promotions that they are executing. This would include special discounts, contests, sweepstakes, coupons, sales, or limited-time product variations. List the promotions that you become aware of in the profile of each competitor.

The final piece of intelligence you will want to gather is the distribution system your competitors use. This has the potential to be an advantage, so it needs to be acknowledged as part of your competitor assessment. Do they use retailers or direct channel? How are they getting their product offering to the customer? Before you wrap up your competitor profiles, learn about their distribution system and use this information in your competitive strategy.

Evaluate Their Operation

Once you have gathered all this intelligence, you can begin to evaluate your competitors. This is where you will transform the information that you have collected about your competitors into the knowledge that you will use to develop a competitive strategy. Your focus will be on what they are doing right, what they're doing wrong, comparing their business to your own, and why they are a threat to you.

Your competitors successes are one of the most important pieces of knowledge that you can gain from your entire evaluation. Of all their operating practices, you want to identify the things that they are doing right. Those strategies and practices that are working for your competitors should be studied so you can plan ways to duplicate them in your own business.

It's always a preferred position to be the pioneer in your industry, but following what has already been proven to work is just smart business. Good strategy is good strategy no matter where it originates. Don't let your pride stop you from implementing winning ideas just because they're not your own. You can still be unique by finding your own way to use the initiatives that you determined are working for your competitors. Go a step further by being better than them at it and " beating them at their own game".

There is also insight to be had when you evaluate your opponents mistakes. Since their successes tell you what your business should be doing, their shortcomings provide examples of what you should stay away from. Whenever possible, learn from your competitors mistakes because making your own is very costly. In this way, knowledge of your competitors strategic errors is hugely valuable.

This new found intimacy with your competitors operations will allow you to compare your businesses. You are trying to assess what it is that they do better than you, and vice versa. Articulate on what makes your companies similar and what makes them different? There's no need to elaborate too much here. A brief, simple comparison will suffice. The point of this is to reveal more about the potential strengths and weaknesses that your organization may have.

The comparison of your business to that of your competitors will also uncover ways that they could potentially threaten you. If you don't want to be caught off-guard, stay prepared for these threats by acknowledging their potential in your competitive analysis. Notate any of the ways that their business may negatively impact your business including loss of market share, loss of customers, or loss of revenues. These negative impacts can result from improvements in their product offerings, new innovations, strategic alliances, increases in operating efficiency, or various other aspects. If any of the threats that you list become a reality, you will want to have a plan of action in place.

Competitive Strategy

At this point, you should have all the intelligence you need to develop a winning strategy. Competing with a specific platform and well-defined protocols ensures that your organization's competitive efforts stay focused. You must plan and know exactly how you will deal with competition, then adhere to the plan and see it through.

If you find flaws in your strategy, or new information is discovered, go ahead and adjust it. In the rare case that your strategy is found to be an absolute failure, then only as a last resort, trash it and devise another. Tried not to totally change strategies too often though, because constant changes and strategic direction that are not healthy for your everyday operation. If you take the time, from the beginning, to carefully craft your strategy and base it with quality information, it should be more than adequate and won't need changing.

Your own competitive strategy may entail any number of elements. You can include whenever intelligence that you feel will help you to compete more effectively. As a standard though there are some common topics that you should consider when developing your competitive game plan like: How will you differentiate your product, how can you steal away market share, how will you handle threats, and ways you can exploit your opponent's weaknesses. These are the elements that will give your strategy a solid foundation.

Product Differentiation

The most basic way to compete is to make your product different, in some form, from the rest of the field. As mentioned before, your product doesn't have to be better than the competitors to be different. It can be similar in function but different in feature. There are a variety of ways to serve the same consumer needs.

Based upon the qualities of the competitions products, strategize how you will differentiate your own. Will you competitively price your product? Will it look different? Will your service be faster? Will your products be exclusive, offering some type of prestige? What exactly will make your offerings unique?

You can differentiate your products on the basis of:

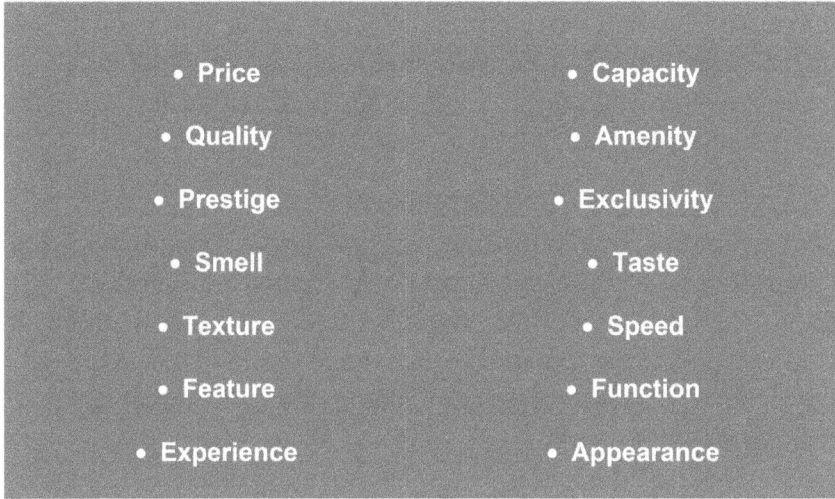

- Price
- Quality
- Prestige
- Smell
- Texture
- Feature
- Experience
- Capacity
- Amenity
- Exclusivity
- Taste
- Speed
- Function
- Appearance

Also emphasize your product's differences on the areas where the competing products lack. If you know that target customers prefer an attribute that your competitor doesn't offer, then use that as a means of differentiation.

Stealing Away Market Share

Normally stealing is absolutely wrong. It is immoral, indecent, and most of all illegal. However, there are specific instances where stealing is acceptable: Stealing a woman's heart, stealing goodies from Grandma's cookie jar, and stealing market share from business competitors. Unfortunately, it is a fact of life that for your business to grow, another must shrink or even fail. Therefore, you have always got to actively pursue your competitor's market share. In your competitive strategy you will detail how you plan to go about taking market share from your competitor.

Stealing market share is really about stealing customers away. The strategy lies in convincing them to stop using your competitors' products and begin using yours. Getting them to consider a change is the first phase, then you've got to persuade them to actually try your product. If your product delivers and proves to be preferable, you may be able to achieve a repeat purchase. This is a major accomplishment and a step towards the ultimate goal: complete conversion. Every customer that you convert over to your product, brings additional sales and revenues which directly translates into increased market share.

To convert customers and steal market share you need to communicate why your product is different and/or better than your competitors. Tell them why they should choose your product. Explain how you can better serve their needs. Express to them the value of making the conversion. You have got to make your competitors' customers feel comfortable and confident about making a change.

In your competitive strategy, explain how you will steal market share. What advertising, promotional, or selling techniques will you use to reach your competitors' customers? Be specific, fully detail your ideas, and diagram your maneuvers.

Handling Threats

You've come to realize how your company will threaten the competition, but how will you prepare for the threats they propose to your enterprise? You can't just bury your head in the sand and hope for the best; you must be proactive and pre-emptive in your approach. When the threats that you predicted before evolve from potential, and start becoming actual, you have got to know what you're going to do.

When your opponent attacks your product with their competitive advertisements, how would you discredit their claims? When they get ready to launch a new product will you unveil yours early to steal their thunder? When they start an effective sales promotion, will you alter your prices temporarily as well? For every action, there is appropriate, counteraction. When your opponent makes a move, be ready to strategically react. This is what competition is all about.

There are an infinite number of possible threats. You will never be able to foresee them all, nor should you try. Just think about any scenario where your competitors pose serious threats to your business. For each of the scenarios, specify your planned course of action.

Exploiting Weaknesses

Earlier you found the weaknesses in your competitor's organization. Exploiting these weaknesses is part of a winning competitive strategy. This refers primarily to their product offering and operation though. In those areas where competitors are the weakest, use your strengths to take advantage. If their service is slow, increase the speed of yours. If their product has a low quality, enhance your products quality. Take the opportunity to further differentiate your products by exploiting the known weaknesses of your competitors.

Explain how you will take advantage of your opponent's weaknesses in your competitive strategy. Talk about each way that you plan to attack their shortcomings. This final piece will sure up your competitive strategy.

Being an effective competitor has the power to bring success to your organization. When you are winning against the competition, your business is usually winning in general. Therefore, it is definitely beneficial for you to devote a significant amount of focus to competing. This will be time well invested.

If you follow these guidelines, you will be able to devise a competitive strategy that will have you legitimately fighting for market share with the best in the field. But no matter how good your competitive strategy is, it should always come second to your overall marketing strategy. You don't want to get so lost in competing that you forget about perfecting your own operation. The main objective has always been, and always will be delivering value to the consumer and serving the demands of the market.

∞

When it comes to the art of competitive intelligence, you are now connoisseur. You have learned how to collect relevant information about the major players in your industry and process it into the knowledge that you will use to create a winning competitive strategy. You are well on your way to becoming a fierce competitor and a real threat to everyone in the market.

Being an effective competitor means nothing if you can't sell the lead once you get it. The opportunity to sell is the culmination of all your marketing efforts. You can't afford to squander any sales opportunities, so therefore in chapter 10, we will focus on crafting a solid sales plan.

Chapter 10:
Marketing Plan Part Seven
Sales Plan

Your phone is ringing off the hook. Your website has significant traffic. Your e-mail inbox overflowing with inquiries. Your shop has people coming through all day. Clearly, your communication efforts are working. But how do you close the deal? How do you turn these leads into sales? You need to develop a sales plan as part of your marketing plan.

When you see a commercial for a beer that you want, you go straight down to the local store and buy a six pack, it's just that simple. In contrast, when you see a commercial for surgical cosmetic procedure that you want, you go through a much more in-depth process a prior to making your purchase. Some product offerings don't need much of a sales plan; they sell themselves through your communication initiatives. Just showing people that the product exists and telling them where to get it is enough. But, other products require more of the hands of one approach. This is where a sales plan can help them to be the most effective at transforming sales leads into done deals.

The sales plan that you write should briefly cover: the sales types you'll use, the procedures within your sales process, the members of your sales team, and your sales goals. These are the elements that will give you the most comprehensive plan. A strong sales plan and strategy will ensure that you get the most out of every sales opportunity. Let's break this down further.

Selling Methods

They say there is more than one way to "skin a cat". Similarly, there is more than one way to sell a product. Each selling method requires a different level of involvement in the sales process. The methods you use will depend on the product you are offering. Typically, to sell bigger ticket or more technical items, you will need to use more elaborate and personal sales methods. These purchases require deeper consideration on behalf of the consumer (or business). Other, more impulse buys can be sold simpler with less involvement.

Possible Selling Methods Include:

- **Brochures/Catalogs** – The least personal selling method. Here, you provide printed materials telling people about the product you're offering and providing them with purchase options (over phone, in store, or by Internet). Printed sales materials can sell the product by themselves or can at least provides some quality leads.

- **Sales Calls** – Making calls to potential customers with the intention of selling your products over the phone. Usually involves some type of call script and sales pitch as part of the strategy. Sales calls can also be used to generate leads or setup sales meetings.

- **Sales Meetings** – The most personal and hands-on sales method. A person-to-person meeting where a product offering is pitched to a prospect. Printed materials, digital visuals, samples, sound bites, simulation models, and other media can be used as sales aides. Negotiating skills may be necessary to close the deal.

- **Infomercial** – Using television or Internet to produce long commercial–like visuals that present, promote, and sell products. Requires a second point of contact (phone, online, male, etc.). To receive orders and processed sales.

- **In–store** – A potential customer comes to the brick–and–mortar location with the intention of making a purchase. A sales representative can be available to assist in the purchase decision, or the display itself can sell the product. This is similar to a sales meeting in–that you have an opportunity to directly interact the customer in–person.

Many times, one sales method alone will not be enough to sell your products. Plan and prepare to use a combination, or all of the sales methods. In the most elaborate sales situations you could mail out brochures to sales leads, then you can make sales calls to those prospects to schedule sales meetings where you will close deals.

Find the best way to use these methods for your particular product offering. Don't try to sell carpet over the phone for example. Expect to meet with the customer bringing samples, pictures, computer models, and any other aid to help you make the sale. As well, you wouldn't set a personal appointment to sell light bulbs (unless you were selling 10,000 units at a time). You will wait for customers to the visit the store. The logical in choosing your selling methods don't waste money or time methods that are in efficient for your product.

Procedure

Selling is a process. It doesn't just happen in one swift move, there are steps to follow. The companies most efficient at selling make it look simple (as if it is done with a single effort) but those on the inside know that it is much more involved. A precise selling procedure must be developed in strictly at here to with every sale.

In most industries, the days of the high-pressure quantity over quality, sales approach are over. Today a smarter and subtler method is favored. Contemporary sales managers have shifted focus on to building a lasting relationship with customers instead of the "one and done" mindset. Sales reps strive to be viewed as consultants rather than greedy, commission-hungry peddlers. They decipher the customer's unique situation and simply offer an advice on how their products can satisfy the needs of the customer.

Selling this way works well because it is highly personal an empathic. Customers don't feel like they are being swindled into yet another purchase that they will later regret. When you can dissipate cognitive dissonance like this, strong relationships can be built and repeat sales are imminent. And we all know that retaining a customer is much cheaper than gaining a new one.

If you want to realize sales success, you'll need to develop your own customer relationship focused sales procedure. This procedure should guide you through the sales process, and result in closed sales at an effective rate. To organize and regiment your selling efforts developing a procedure is necessary.

The steps in your sales procedure must cover some semblance of the following: lead generation, pre–sale techniques, sales pitch, sale–closing strategies, and post-sale techniques. Each of these functions (arranged in ascending order) are integral parts to a consistently effective sales process. With a specified procedure in place you'll be able to adequately train your sales staffs to not only more units but produce value for every customer.

Generating Leads

The first step to any sales situation is finding leads. A lead is defined as some entity (individual or business) bead for your product, some interest in your product, and the means to purchase your product. Simply put, a lead is a potential buyer.

Leads can be found anywhere and everywhere if your eyes are open to the opportunities. Leads are generated through referrals, networking, solicitation responses, mailing lists, cold calling, and others. It is only a matter of where you choose to look.

Some tactics produce better quality leads than others based on their nature. Referrals bring the best quality leads because the prospect trusts the referring source; therefore, the prospect already has a favorable impression of your product offering. Cold calls generally yield leads with less potential because the lead is most likely unfamiliar with you and your product offering. The catch is, referrals are usually rare and harder to come by, while cold calls can be made by anyone at any time. No matter where the lead comes from, it will have some potential to be converted into a sale.

The best quality leads have the highest conversion rates. For example, a prospect who inquires about your product based on an advertisement that they seen (higher quality lead) are more likely to buy then someone contacted off of a mailing list (lower-quality lead). In the example, the prospect that is contacting you is already interested in your product on some level, and it's prime to purchase. In-contrast, the prospect that you contact from a mailing list is caught off guard and was not pondering a purchase at the time. It must be additionally noted that bringing in leads from solicitation responses or referrals are harder to obtain than simply purchasing a mailing list containing hundreds or thousands of names.

You will find it necessary to get your leads from several sources. Collect leads from the places that make the most sense for your company and your product offering. Your goal is to sustain a continuous inflow of good quality leads as efficiently as possible. In your sales procedure, just specify how you plan to generate the leads that will provide your sales opportunities.

Pre-Sale Techniques

Before you dive in headfirst and start soliciting your leads, there's a few things you should do first. To improve your conversion rate, it's best to plan some pre-sale techniques and yourself procedure. Invest the time to qualify your leads, profile your prospects, and plan your approach, and you will find yourself in excellent position to close a large number of your sales.

One way to enhance the quality of a lead is to qualify them prior to devoting resources into a sales attempt. It is an extremely inefficient waste of time trying to sell to someone who can't even afford your product. For this reason, every lead on your list should be pre-qualified. You must be sure that each lead has an actual need for your product offering, is receptive to your sales pitch, can be accessed, and has the ability to purchase. Any lead that can't meet these requirements should be eliminated and removed from your list. These are not true leads and are not worth the sales effort.

Another important presale technique is profiling your prospects. The more you know about them the better. In chapter 7 you profiled your target markets, but that was on more of a macro and generalist level. Here, you want to get as personal and individualistic as possible, especially when your list of leads is smaller. As you are profiling prospects, you should focus on assessing their specific needs, identifying their problems, and noting their interests. You will find this information to be priceless later in the sales process.

With your leads qualified and adequately profiled, you can plan your approach. This is just another way for you to prepare yourself (or your sales team) to make a sale. Each sales situation is different, and you must treat it that way. The information that you have collected so far you will use to strategize the best way to approach each unique lead. Think about what your angle will be. Consider how you will relate to the prospect. Plan to express exactly how you are going to fulfill their needs and solve their problem. Next, you will make your move.

Sales Pitch

At this point in the procedure you are ready to present your sales pitch to potential customers. This is where the actual art of the sale will take place. If your pre-sale techniques were adequate, then your prospects should be well primed and ready for your approach.

The sales message that you deliver has to be fundamentally consistent, even though each of your leads will be unique. The attributes and features of your product will provide a basis for your sales message, because these don't change. These are selling points. In every sales situation you will explain to the prospect what your product is, what it does, and how it works. But, to appeal to the prospect on an individual level, you will also explain how the prospect will personally benefit by purchasing your product. This is what pitching is: showing leads how the basic elements of your product offering will enhance their lives personally; expressing the value of your product.

When you are in a sales meeting or selling over the phone, you are going to need prepared selling points and an overall sales message to operate from. This is very important to your sales procedure, because it gives your presentation continuity and structure. The sales message you develop will be like the script that keeps your presentation on track.

The strength of your presentation will depend largely on the effectiveness of your sales message. Carefully consider what selling points you will emphasize to best convey the value of your products. As part of yourselves procedure create a document with all of your selling points and modem into an overall sales message. Use it as a template to guide you through every sales pitch opportunity.

Sale Closing Strategies

Conversions...That's the objective of the entire selling process. Converting is turning potential customers into actual customers. It is where leads cross the threshold from just being interested to being ready to buy. Before you can achieve conversions, you will need to employ some sale - closing strategies in your sales opportunities. These tactics are designed to help your leads make the decision to purchase.

And the pitching phase of the sales procedure you presented prospects with all of the pertinent information about your product offering. You began to create value in their minds. In this phase, true persuasion takes place, and you will continue building up their perception of value. The art of the sale intensifies here.

One of the most classic clothing strategies is overcoming objections. Sales people frequently hone this skill, because they know that almost every prospect will have some type of objection to a sales pitch. It is rare that a person will be prepared to buy immediately following a sales presentation. They will have objections. We have become skeptical creatures by nature, and we will find reasons why we should keep our money instead of spending it. If your sales people give up after one objection, you will never make any sales. They must be ready to overcome at least a few objections to close deals.

Now let's be clear, overcoming objections does not necessarily mean apply pressure to the sale situation. In most cases, high-pressure selling can backfire. It makes prospects feel cornered and apprehensive. If they do buy, it's usually in smaller quantities, and their level of cognitive dissonance is elevated. Pressure is not the point here, it is counterproductive. Handling objections is about answering questions and addressing concerns in an attempt to assist your lead in moving towards a decision.

Another part of closing sales is negotiation. This won't come into play in all sales situations, but it's a strategy worth exploring. If the lead agrees to buy, you may need to negotiate price, warranties, deliveries, service plans, or other terms. To get the outcome that is favorable for you, but also satisfying to your customer, will take some level of negotiation.

Get prepared to negotiate by knowing what your flexibility is exactly. Understand your limits! Decide what you are willing to concede, and what you will expect in return. Whenever you give something in a negotiation, you should always get something back. For example, if you give a discount, ask for early payment. If you give a free gift, ask for a referral. When your customer starts negotiating, don't get caught off guard. Be prepared! Negotiation is the conclusion of your sale.

Post-Sale Techniques

Every time you close a sale, you should be immediately thinking about shoring up future sales with current customers. Remember...Your sales procedure is designed to build relationships with those who purchase your product. These relationships are cultivated in the post-sale phase of the sales process. Taking care of the customer after the sale is almost as important as the sale itself.

Post-sale techniques are all about retention. You are trying to retain your customers by ensuring their satisfaction and keeping them happy. This is done by following up with them, immediately and fully rectifying any problems that arise, and just being there as a pillar of support. When customers know that you value them in this way, they will return.

If not enough for your customer to be satisfied with just the product itself; you want them to be satisfied with the entire purchase experience. A large part of this experience occurs post purchase. Checking up on your customers shows them that you care about them, and not just their money. When you ask them if everything was okay with the product, or request additional feedback, it lets them know that you care about quality and providing the best product possible. As a bonus, following up creates an opportunity for you to solicit another purchase.

Customer service after the sale builds the perception of total value. And when your customers feel like they've received adequate value for their money they will spend more of it with you. This is the point of post-sale techniques.

In your sales procedure specify your post sell tactics. How long after purchase before you follow up? How will you follow up (call, email, postcard, etc.)? What kind of support will you provide? how will you invite them to make another purchase? Explain how you are going to care for your customers and maintain a good standing relationship with them.

Your sales procedure concludes with post sale activities. When properly planned and executed, the end of your sales procedure can also be the beginning of a new sales cycle. The process will start over again, but the next time it will be much more expedient and simpler for both parties. Your entire procedure should be designed to promote cyclical selling like this as opposed to straight-line (a straight line has a beginning and end; a cycle is continuous). If you plan your sales procedures with a focus on establishing connections, and relating to people, not only will your conversion rate flourish, but your level of retention will be exceptional as well.

Sales Team

Who is going to sell your product offering? This is prime information for your sales plan. Your salesforce can take many different forms. You might start off doing all the work yourself, but at some point, in your company's evolution, you may need some additional assistance. If you have to establish a sales team you will plan for it here.

When planning for your sales team think about what your

particular needs are or will be. The more "self-selling" your product is, the less of a sales team you need. As mentioned before, items that are inexpensive and purchased without much thought will sell themselves. Your only concern here is persuading retailers to carry them, if you choose that route. Items that require a more complex sales effort may need a team dedicated to fulfilling the tasks related to moving these products.

Depending on the depth of your sales procedure your plan can include a team that handles telemarketing (cold calling, lead generating, lead qualifying); sales presentations (including closing); and post-sale initiatives. You can have a different team responsible for each phase of your sales procedure, or one team that handles the entire sales process from induction to closing. Divide labor however you see fit.

Also consider how your teams will be constructed. Specify what job titles are necessary, and how you will fill these positions. The bigger your team grows, the more management is needed, address this concern as well. Basically, who will be responsible for what? Make sure that every task within your sales process is covered.

Finally, think about the compensation package that you will offer to the members of your sales team. It's important for you to know if you will pay them on a commission basis, hourly basis, or both. Each of these pay structures has a unique impact on performance. Commission rewards performance, while hourly promotes loyalty and provide stability for the sales team employees. Commission requires less of a commitment on the employer's part because you don't have to pay until a sale is made. In contrast, compensating on an hourly basis builds goodwill because it shows faith in the employee. With this being said, it is suggested that you construct a compensation plan that combines both pay structures in some way.

Your Sales Goals

The final piece of your sales plan is setting your goals. No matter what type of product you sell, or how in-depth yourself procedure is, you need to have specific goals for yourselves initiatives to aim for. Creating these measures will provide you with a level of quantification that you can use to ensure your sales efforts are progressing adequately.

The goals you choose should be a microcosm of your organizational objectives. Each sales goal should advance you closer towards your ultimate company goals--positive cash flows and consistent growth! if you have taken the time to create meaningful objectives (see chapter 4 "Projected Future" section) then you will know exactly what benchmarks you need to reach to achieve your projected market share, revenue, and growth aims. If you find your company heading towards these objectives then you are doing the right things, if not, then you need to make adjustments to your methods.

And include several different types of measurements encompassing every component of your sales process. These goals will be numerical and nature and can be based on the most detail statistics (like number of leads generated or calls made per week) up to the more significant measures (like conversion rate, units sold, or sales revenue). Remember, quality goals will be specific, time-sensitive, and most-of-all attainable.

You may have already set up some of your major sales goals in section one of your marketing plan. If so, in the sales plan portion focus on the details. Express to your sales team exactly what is expected of them by setting goals for every step of your sales procedure. Tell them how many leads need to be generated, how many leads needs to be qualified, how many calls to make, and so on. This way, you walk them through the smaller goals that lead up to the larger actual selling based goals. Further, there will be no misunderstandings, and everyone knows what they need to do to satisfy their obligations.

As you become more experienced in your process, you will become more aware of what to expect from your particular operation. You will learn the average response rate to your communication efforts. Of those who take action and respond you will learn the average amount who actually convert into paying customers. Some will convert on the first contact, while others will require several contacts. Certain targets will be more responsive through email communication, then through a phone call. The more of this kind of information you collect in your trials, the better your goals will be, mostly because they will be realistic and reachable.

As a final tip, consider setting your goals just outside of reach. That is, make the goals reachable with extra effort, but unlikely to achieve with normal effort. Packages from here depending on the personalities of your sales team members, this technique has strong motivational abilities because they will hate just getting close to the goal, but never reaching it. The most driven members on your team will overachieve to realize these goals, and everyone else will look to follow the in their footsteps.

Finish off your sales plan with a solid goal structure and you'll be well on your way towards building stable cash flows. Sales goals provide at destination to be reached, keeps your sales department looking in front of them instead of behind, and demands they continue moving forward. Sales goals illuminate the steps on the path to prosperity. With quality statistical data and quantifiable performance expectations, your organization's advancement is imminent.

∞

A well-constructed and comprehensive sales plan allows you to attack the market with some consistency. Your sales plan should lead you to the formula that gives the best conversion rates. You will then use this formula to close a sale after sale on your way towards meeting (or exceeding) your sales goals. Reaching these goals mean increased sales, which ultimately means enhanced levels of cash flow, our overall objective.

In the very first chapter, we discussed the importance of cash flow. Since then, we haven't really talked about it much. A large portion of the next chapter is devoted to cash flow. Will cover various subtopics related to cash flow to get a good understanding of how to manage it properly. The chapter will conclude by elaborating on how to complete a cash flow projection and budgeting.

Chapter 11
Marketing Plan Part Eight:
Cash Flow Statements and Budgets

Everything you've done so far has lead up to this. Establishing your company, perfecting your product offering, identifying your targets, building your brand, designing and executing marketing campaigns, sizing up the competition, creating a sales protocol, and all your other planning activities are meant to do one thing, bring in cash! Without a positive inflow of cash, nothing else is possible. To be brutally honest, a business that cannot consistently produced a net positive cash flow is a failure, pure and simple.

With all the other elements of your marketing plan decided, you can began forecasting the expected cash flow from your business operations. This will include positive cash flow as well as negative cash flow. You must consider both because every action, every procedure, every business practice your organization engages in will either directly cost you money or make you money. In this section you'll do your best to account for each dollar that you expect to flow through your business according to your model. These forecasts will be the truest test of your marketing plans feasibility. If you can honestly prove that your business – as constructed – is capable of generating net positive cash flow, it will be a good indicator that you are on the right track.

Here also, if you will develop budgets for the various divisions of your operation. If you don't cap your spending, it can quickly get out of hand. Therefore, a good quality budget protocol is just as important as a strong goal structure. Just as goal setting checks progress, budgets check spending. In this chapter you learn how to complete relevant budgets and the most practical way.

Cash Flow Basics

We will examine cash flow and its entirety, but first let's get an understanding of exactly what cash is.

More Than Just Paper

To most of us, cash is thought of only in the sense of green paper or coins. While these currencies are the most traditional types of cash, they are not the only types. Cash comes in many forms.

The term cash refers to any liquid asset. An asset is liquid when it is easily converted into actual currency. Liquid assets include: bank transfers, checks (all types), money orders, securities (stocks, bonds, commissary notes), bit coins, precious metals, and any other liquid item of value. Things like real estate, vehicles, equipment, or inventories are not considered as cash because turning them into usable currency usually takes more time and effort.

How does Cash Flow Work?

In its most simple definition, cash flow is the movement of cash through your business. In the everyday operation of your organization, there will be money coming in and going out. You will spend money keeping your organization operational, and the result should be closed sales which is the money coming in. Any transaction that either cost cash or produces cash is considered part of the cash flow.

Envision your company's checking account when thinking about cash flow. Withdrawals debit the account, taking money out.

Deposits credit the account, putting money in. Each of these actions will affect the amount of usable cash at your disposal.

As you have probably guessed, cash inflows are positive and cash outflows are negative. Inflows are positive because they add cash to the balance. Cash outflows are negative because a subtract funds from the cash balance. They each originate from different occurrences in your business practice, but they work together.

Positive and Negative

Positive cash flow derives from revenues (income from sales) direct returns on investment, or capital borrowed from lenders. When people buy your products and they pay in cash (paper currency, bank transfer, or electronic) positive cash flow is created. Investments your company makes that produce positive returns (in the form of interests earned, dividends received, or liquidation) produce cash inflow. Despite the fact that they must be paid back, funds acquired from lenders provide inflows as well. Accounts receivable is also considered positive cash flow because even though they are credit purchases, they still are purchases, and the promissory notes are liquid assets. Each of these activities bring money into your organization.

Negative cash flow is sourced from not only expenses, but also payments and investments. Officially, expenses are the costs of the goods and services associated with operating an enterprise (cost of goods sold, waged expense, rent, advertising, and so on). Payments are cash outflows that are dedicated to satisfying debt obligations. Investments come out of the cash balance, and are used to purchase investment instruments like securities, new equipment, additional inventory, or even the entire business acquisitions. Each of these transactions debit your company's cash account.

They Work Together

As mentioned earlier, positive and negative cash flow work in conjunction with one another. One cannot exist without the other; they form a ying and yang of sorts. There is no such thing as a business that produces only positive cash flow unless someone figured out how to sell us the outside air. It will always cost money to bring money in.

Even though cash outflows are thought of as negative, they are absolutely necessary and just as important as cash inflows. As a matter of fact, negative cash flow starts the cash flow cycle. This is because cash outflows are an investment in gaining inflows. Any time you spend money operating your business it is with the intention of making more back. If everything works the way it's supposed to, you will bring in sales revenue (inflow). Then, a percentage of this inflow is reinvested into the business as outflow, and the cycle is perpetuated.

Net-Positive Cash Flow

The bottom line... You can't have more going out then coming in. Similarly, you also can't have your positive and negative cash flow equal each other. The former is net - negative, while the latter is net-neutral. Neither is sustainable for your organization. If you want to stay in business, your cash flow must be net-positive. This is the only successful configuration.

Net-positive means that your cash in-flows exceed your cash outflows. After subtracting all of your negative transactions from your positive transactions over a given period, you want the resulting number to be positive. This means that your business model is working because you are profiting! the next question is how can you increase this? Bring in more cash?

Increasing your positive cash flow is always a good thing, but it is only half of the equation when it comes to improving your bottom line. There are many companies that have truckloads of revenues, but busloads of costs and expenses to match. It doesn't matter how much you bring in if you can't control what is going out. That is the other half of our equation, control outflow.

For example, company A (a small company) has cash inflow of $54,000 for the year, and cash outflow of $30,000; giving them a net positive cash balance of $24,000 for the year. Company B have a good night good nice day (the larger competitor of company A) has $240,000 of positive cash flow for the year with $180,000 of negative cash flow, providing a $60,000 net positive cash balance. It is obvious which company have more cash in the year, but which is more efficient?

Company A brings in $16 for every $10 it spends (a net positive return of 60% on each dollar spent). Company B earns only $13.40 for every $10 its spends (a 33.3% net-positive return). Even though company B brought and more than double the net positive cash flow that company A brought in, company A appears to be more efficiently operated. How do we know this? because according to the numbers company A is doing a better job controlling their negative cash flow in proportion to their positive cash flow. Now this is the only measure of efficiency, and there are many other variables we could consider, but for our purposes we are keeping it simple and concluding that company A is more efficient.

Improving your net positive cash flow means you must minimize negative cash flow while maximizing positive cash flow. You have to figure out how to make more money with less spending. Easier said than done right? Part of your organization's natural progression is to become more efficient as you become more experienced in operating your business. But you will have to stay proactive and diligent and continuously looking for ways to reduce outflows while enhancing inflows.

Cash Flow Statements

With a good working knowledge of cash flow, you can begin forecasting your cash flow potential. Your forecast will materialize in the form of a cash flow statement. The cash flow statement is an accounting of all the actions expected to affect the cash account of your business. It reports all collections and payments over a given period.

You will use your other financial projections to also forecast your expected cash flow over at least a 12-month span. With your sales goals quantified, you can calculate the corresponding cash inflow that will result from these sales. The estimated expenses and costs required to achieve these cells can be easily calculated as your outflows. Then, you can subtract your projected outflows from your projected inflows to forecast your potential net cash flow.

In your marketing plan include a cash flow forecast to give yourself an extended view of your expected cash situation. You want to get some idea of what you expect to be going out and what you expect to be coming back in. As you are putting together your forecasted cash flow statement be sure to use only the most accurate figures you can fathom. Many times, planners tend to overstate positive cash flows. Don't fall into this trap. Unrealistic estimates will render your forecast useless.

The cash flow statement is best interpreted when it is divided into months. It has several different measures. The headings of each section include:

- **Beginning Cash Balance:** The amount of cash your company has at the month's beginning.

- **Positive Cash Flows (or Inflows):** The cash that is coming into your business. This includes income from sales, accounts receivable, and lines of credit that have been drawn from.

- **Total Positive Cash Flows:** The sum of all cash inflows over a period.

- **Negative Cash Flows (or Inflows):** The cash going out of your business to be spent running it. This includes new asset purchases, inventory replenishments, investments, and loss of sales.

- **Operating Activities:** A negative cash flow category that accounts for the costs associated with operations like salaries, fixed business expenses, and taxes.

- **Financing Activities:** Another negative cash flow category that accounts for the cash allocated to satisfying debts. Within this category is loan payments, interest expense, line of credit repayments, or dividends paid.

- **Total Negative Cash Flows:** The sum of all the cash outflows including the negative cash flow category, the operating activities category, and the financing activities category.

- **Net Cash Flow:** The calculated difference between the total positive cash flows and total net cash flows.

- **Operating Cash Balances:** The net cash flow added to the beginning cash balance.

After completing an honest forecast, examine the results. In the first couple of months you may come out with an even or slightly negative, cash balance as you work to build up your revenue. But, you should see some progression as the months go along. If your projections calculate to a consistently net negative flow though, it is an indication that you may need to rethink your business model. It may also be the case that your business model is fine and you just need to secure a line of credit temporarily to supplement your cash balance until you can improve your operating efficiency by increasing revenues and/or decreasing costs.

The cash flow statement is not only a valuable forecasting tool; it also provides an important benchmark for all your planning efforts. You can use your cash flow forecast to check the accuracy of your financial projections (sales, costs, expenses, etc.) once you start operating in the real world. This means, you should be using cash flow statements, much in the same way that you used it for forecasting.

After recording your actual numbers, you will be able to compare them to your forecasted numbers to measure your progress towards meeting these goals. Was your inflow what you expected? Was your outflow what you expected? How close were your projections? As an added bonus, the real-time cash flow figures you collect will be useful in helping you to improve the accuracy of your future financial projections.

A true understanding of the cash flow concept will help you to enhance your cash flow potential and operating efficiency. While it is preferable to be able to achieve and maintain higher volumes of cash flow, your focus must be on maximizing net positive cash flow no matter the volume. It does you no good to have a $1,000,000 coming in if you have $999,000 going back out. Your business can't grow like that. If you apply what you have learned here about cash flow you will be able to continuously improve your positive to negative cash flow ratio.

The cash flow statement keeps all your movements in check. The forecast version sets the parameters, while the actual record accounts for each and every cash transaction. Through the cash statement, you will be able to responsibly monitor your cash flows, and keep the books balanced on your cash account. With your cash movements under control in this way, your chances of mismanagement decreased greatly.

Budgeting

Picture for a moment you are in line at the grocery store. Your cart is full of healthy items from the five food groups, and maybe a few not so healthy choices from the lesser acknowledged food group: Desert...Mmm. This has been a wonderful experience so far because you shopped without a conscience. You picked everything you thought looked good and just threw it in the cart.

You reach the front of the line with a big smile on your face, obviously satisfied with your selections. You've done well for yourself. Your mouth is watering from the thoughts of all the scrumptious meals you will be able to make once you get home.

The cashier sighs at the sight of your goliath purchase but begins scanning your items anyway. As your order is processed through the computer and bagged, you watch eagerly, totally oblivious to the accumulating price. After scanning what seemed like an endless conveyor belt of items, the cashier recites your monumental total. Gladly, you dig into your pockets to pay your bill, but when you find your wad of cash (let's pretend it's 1992 and people still use cash) you quickly realize is too small. You can't afford even half this order!

At this point, you are not only disappointed because you have to return many of your selections; but you are also embarrassed because the cashiers visibly frustrated with you. What a disaster! but what happened? A simple failure to budget. You spent more than you had.

In the future, you will probably be aware of exactly how much you have to spend before making a trip to the market. Further, you will know exactly what needs to be purchased with what you have to spend. You may even take it a step further and compile an itemized list that you will stick to. In essence, prior to going shopping, you will create a budget to regulate your spending.

Budgeting in your business is just as important (if not more important) as budgeting in your personal life. If you overextend your means in one area, other areas will suffer. Overspending at the grocery store may result in a lack of funds to pay the electric bill which keeps the refrigerator running. Similarly, in your business, if you overspend on wages, you may not have the means to pay the lease on your office building, which houses your employees. Developing budgets is an absolute necessity for conducting and efficient and fiscally responsible business.

Budgeting is just another monetary control method. It helps you to become a discipline spender. When you have a tight budget looming over your head, you are more apt to make better purchase decisions with less waste. You will be able to disseminate between what you can afford and what you cannot afford. The parameters set by a good budget encourages you to satisfy your needs but dissuades you from doing it with frivolous spending. Adhering closely to a well-written budget allows you to get the most utility from every dollar that flows out of your business

Every division of your operation you're spending takes place will need its own budget. This includes startup costs, R&D (Research and Development), advertising, public relations, promotion, and general operations. Each of the sections will command a different portion of your overall outgoing funds; therefore, it is imperative that you know how much capital you plan to devote to each section. Developing budgets is how you will correctly allocate your funds amongst the elements of your operations.

Establishing general spending caps is a good start, which you can take it a step further. The components within each division can have their own smaller budget as a part of the division. For example, you may have developed a particular advertising campaign and given it a budget of $10,000. Within this budget, you will need to allot the amounts that will be spent on the different forms of advertising you planned as part of the campaign.

Example:
Advertising Campaign A: Budget $10,000

- Television ads - $5,000

- Print ads - $2,000

- Internet ads - $1,000

- Radio ads - $2,000

Using the categories in the above example, the $5,000 television advertising budget for instance, could be split into two amounts that will be spent buying slots on certain days, times, or channels. You can be as meticulous as you want with your budgeting. Remember, the more detailed your budgets are, the more control you have over your spending.

You also want to consider time frame when you are creating budgets. Over what span of time will you exhaust this budget? How long is this budget good for? Staying with the above example, the $10,000 "Campaign A" budget could be a monthly budget, a quarterly budget, or even the year's budget. Once again, it is in your best interest to break the time frame down to lower terms. If $10,000 is the annual budget, then it should be divided into shorter periods upon which adherence to the budget can be consistently checked. Placing time constraints on your budgets makes them more specific and quantifiable.

Each division will have its own set of tasks that you must budget for.

- **Start-up Costs:** When you are first starting your business, it is vitally important to adhere to a budget because your funds will be limited. Here, you will need to budget for things like building (leased or purchase), supplies, beginning inventory, equipment, website design, covering initial operating expenses (for at least 6 months), and others.

- **Research and Development:** when you are trying to collect market information, and/ or create a new product offering. It is easy to overspend while chasing perfection. It is understandable because money spent on R&D will be the best investment you make into your business. Included in this budget will be procurements like market research, market testing, product research, product design, product testing, equipment purchases, and other elements related to R&D.

- **Advertising:** Getting the word out about your business or product offering is vital to your success, but if not kept in check with a budget, advertising costs can get out of hand and empty your bank account quickly. Your overall advertising budget will cover all the different advertising vehicles (print, television, radio, internet) you plan to use, as well as the costs associated with developing and designing these ads.

- **Public Relations:** Shaping public perceptions is not the most expensive communication method but it still has some costs. If you don't want to spend too much, you need to budget for research expenditures, press release writing, consulting fees, press release distribution, event planning, donations, newsletter creation, sponsorships, and others.

- **Promotions:** Promotional budgets experience the most pressure because they cover a wide range of activities. There are a variety of ways to promote your business, and each that you plan to use in your campaigns must be carefully budgeted for so that you can clearly define your limits. Expect things like giveaways, free samples, lost revenue on discounts or sales, event planning, displays, trial, demonstrations, and more to be a part of your promotional budget.

- **General Operation:** You must keep a handle on the expenses you incur in the everyday operation of your business as well. Even though they appear in small increments, your operational expenses can add up fast. To operate most efficiently, you have to "cut the fat" from your fixed operating expenses. Do this by developing the tightest possible budget for costs like: energy (not related to production), office supplies, banking fees, travel expenses, administrative, wages, storage fees (physical and electronic), janitorial maintenance, and anything else that you can manipulate.

Staying on Budget

Once you develop budgets for all the different segments of your operation how do you stay true to them? Easier said than done. In the real world, budgets provide excellent guidelines for you to follow, but sometimes it can be difficult to stay within their parameters. Unexpected changes, miscalculations, catastrophic events, desire to indulge, and other circumstances can easily derail your efforts to stay on track. To consistently adhere to your budgets, you must remain within the principle of the three D's: diligence, discipline, and discretion.

Diligence is what keeps you focused and determined to stay on budget. You will always be cognizant of where you're spending is in relation to the budget. For example, it's time for you to shop for office supplies. Because you are diligent, you break down your monthly supplies budget into a detailed list of all the items you need to purchase and how much you plan to spend on each before you begin shopping. This attention to detail helps you follow the budget. Additionally, a diligent business owner scrutinizes all spending activities with a fine-tooth comb to spot inefficiencies and eliminate waste.

To use **discretion** is to be responsible with your spending. This means that when you are faced with one of your daily spending decisions you make the choice that's best for the budget, even when it's hard. Let's say, for example, that your best employee asks for a raise in her salary. You would love to give it to her because you know she deserves it, but you also know that it will put you grossly over your current operating budget. Since you can't immediately afford to adjust the budget, unfortunately, you must deny her the raise at that time and try to find another way to compensate her (maybe stock options, promise of a future raise, or discounts on company merchandise). Discretionary spending is no nonsense and sometimes harsh, but it forces you to be creative and think pragmatically to satisfy your needs.

Discipline is probably the most important budget adherence trait. Without discipline, you can find yourself breaking the budget every time it's convenient. In many ways, being on a budget is like being on a diet. To avoid the temptation to cheat on your diet (by eating that piece of red velvet cake) requires a significant amount of discipline. Similarly, stopping yourself from overspending your budget on that more comfortable, but too expensive, new office chair also takes discipline. Controlling yourself in the face of temptation is not always easy, but if you stay disciplined in your spending, you will stay on budget.

A few other ways to save money and/or avoid breaking budget are:

- **Controlling Turnover:** For businesses with employees, turnover can be one of the biggest budget busters. The process of interviewing, hiring, and training new employees has astronomical costs. The more you spend here, the less you will have to spend on other important business initiatives. Therefore, it is only in your best interest to control turnover with a human resource policy that not only brings in the best people, but also retains them for as long as possible. This will help you to save loads on your operating budget.

- **Outsourcing:** There are instances where it's much more economical for you to pay others to complete jobs for you as opposed to doing them in house. If you do some research, you will find that other companies are sometimes better qualified and more efficient at certain tasks than you are. And these cases it may be cheaper to just hire them. finding the right places to outsource labor, can save you tons of money making it easier to stay on budget.

- **Find Cheaper, but Adequate Alternatives:** Sometimes when you are in a budget crunch, you will have to make some adjustments. In order to afford everything, you require you may find some less expensive alternatives to some of the things you need. What's important though is that the alternatives you choose can adequately fulfill your needs.

- **Remove the Fluff:** Your budgets need to be lean as possible. Analyze them to find any areas where you may be able to make cuts. It's like looking for the quickest path to a destination. Anything in your budget that is not absolutely necessary to complete your objective should be eliminated. If you find some extra moving room (money) this way you can use it to extend another budget or add the savings to your bottom line.

∞

The everyday conducting of your business and selling of your product offering creates cash flow through your operation. Unless your cash flow ends up net positive at the end of the period, you've done something wrong. Maintaining a net positive cash flow requires a focus on minimizing the money going out while maximizing the money coming in. This can be done by controlling outflows with budgeting. Finally, no matter how good a budget is, it can only be effective when it is actually followed with religious conviction.

Forecasting your cash flow potential provide you with important benchmarks to reach for as you start conducting business. It shows you what the measure of success is. Recording your actual cash flow indicates your proximity to that measure of success in real time. As you record more real-time data, a pattern begins to develop, and a standard appears. You will learn what cash flow you can normally expect. With this standard revealed, it will become clear what it takes to exceed the standard and grow your business.

An honest cash flow forecast and spending budget completes your marketing plan. This is the test of the viability of your business concept. If you can find enough positive cash flow in your forecast in a short time span, then chances are you've got a winning formula.

Now, the only thing that's left to do is to take your plans and start walking down your path to prosperity!